50
MOSAIC MURALS

50
MOSAIC MURALS

DECORATIVE MOSAIC ART FOR THE HOME

TERESA MILLS

Illustrations by John and Carol Woodcock

NEW BURLINGTON BOOKS

A QUARTO BOOK

Published by New Burlington Books
6 Blundell Street
London N7 9BH

ISBN 13: 978-1-84566-224-0

QUAR. MMU

Conceived, designed, and produced by
Quarto Publishing plc
The Old Brewery
6 Blundell Street
London N7 9BH

Project Editor: **Lindsay Kaubi**
Designer: **Karin Skånberg**
Illustrators: **John Woodcock, Carol Woodcock**
Text Editor: **Fiona Plowman**
Assistant Art Directors: **Penny Cobb, Caroline Guest**
Photographer: **Martin Norris**
Proofreader: **Sue Viccars**
Indexer: **Helen Snaith**

Art Director: **Moira Clinch**
Publisher: **Paul Carslake**

Manufactured by PICA Digital, Singapore
Printed by Star Standard Industries (PTE) Ltd, Singapore

1 3 5 7 9 10 8 6 4 2

CONTENTS

MOSAIC DIRECTORY

LIVING SPACE

SUNROOM

KITCHEN

BATHROOM

BEDROOM

NURSERY

INTRODUCTION

YOU NEED A CERTAIN AMOUNT OF CONFIDENCE–AND TIME–TO UNDERTAKE A MOSAIC MURAL. THE RESULTS HOWEVER CAN BE VERY REWARDING, NOT JUST THE FINISHED PIECE, BUT ALSO THE PROCESS ITSELF. CUTTING AND LAYING THE PIECES OF A MOSAIC IS UNIQUELY ABSORBING: YOU WILL FIND IT BOTH INTENSE AND RELAXING AT THE SAME TIME.

Creating a mosaic mural is a unique challenge and before undertaking a full-sized project, you will need to consider where you are going to site it and how the colors will work with your existing decor. A mural may be "bold and busy," suited to more colorful rooms, for example complementing the chaos of a child's bedroom, or a bathroom or kitchen with an equally bright color scheme. Alternatively, a design might provide a subtle but effective point of interest in an otherwise plain area such as a hallway or stairwell. With this in mind the designs in this book have been organized according to suggested location; however many of them would work in any room in the house.

None of the designs in the book is set in stone. You can rearrange or combine elements from different murals and the final color palette you choose is entirely up to you.

Before you begin, read, understand, and practice the techniques described in the first section. This takes you through the materials you will need, how to prepare a baseboard, scaling and transferring your design, grouting, and, importantly, the different types of tiles you can use and how to cut and place these consistently and accurately. This is the central skill of creating mosaics, and if you practice nothing else in advance of undertaking a project then concentrate on the use of your tile nippers until you can confidently turn a tile piece into exactly the shape the design demands. This section also provides information on finishing

ABOUT THIS BOOK

The materials you will need and the best tools for the job are described on pages 10–13. Basic skills and core techniques, including cutting tiles, preparing surfaces, gluing and grouting, scaling and transferring, and mounting and finishing can be found on pages 14–23. The Mosaic Directory starts on page 24.

Mosaic Directory

The mural designs in the Mosaic Directory have been designed to give you the maximum assistance in creating a beautiful finished result. Some of the designs feature panoramic murals on fold-out flaps.

Each mosaic has a suggested order of work; generally, the best practice is to start with central details and then work outward, finishing with any larger, flat areas of color in the background.

Each project shows the design on a grid to make it easy to scale and transfer the design to your baseboard.

Each design is shown in two possible colorways. You can choose the one you prefer, or create your own unique mix of colors.

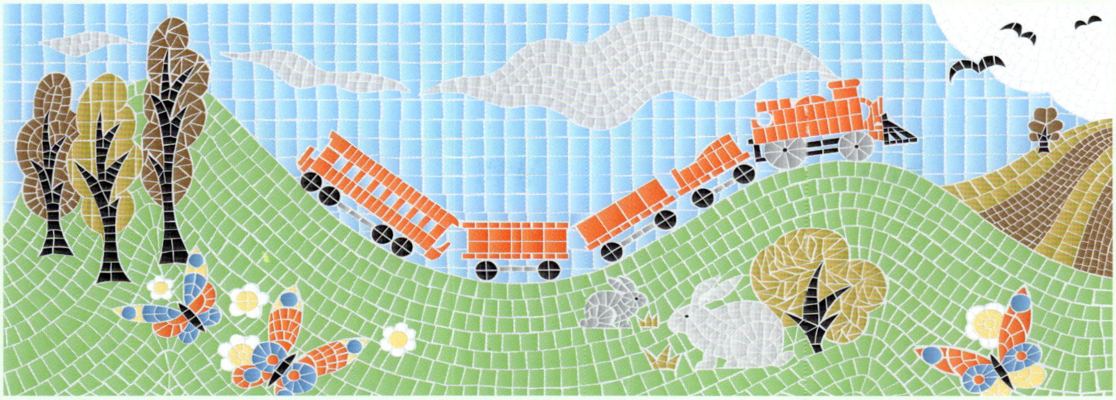

and mounting a completed design. This is particularly important because the finished pieces can be very heavy and must be mounted properly otherwise they could be dangerous.

If you are new to mosaics, you should probably start off by working on a small area of one or two of the designs from the Mosaic Directory, so as to understand and practice the core techniques of mosaic that are described in the techniques section.

Mosaic skills are based on the three "p"s: pincers, practice, and, above all, patience. Treat each piece like a jigsaw—you need to look at each tile carefully and cut and "nibble" with your pincers until it fits—avoid the temptation to squeeze things in, or to be content with tile fragments that are "nearly" right.

It only remains to be said that I hope you find the projects in this book pleasurable and rewarding to do. The mural designs are intended to suit a wide range of tastes; there is something here for everyone. I hope you enjoy making them as much as I have enjoyed designing them, and that this book provides a way into this beautiful and ancient decorative art form, which has so many possibilities.

TERESA MILLS

All the murals can be completed with standard vitreous mosaic tiles or ordinary household tiles cut to size; in some cases we indicate which is most suitable.

Information on the finished size is included in order to optimize the use of tiles.

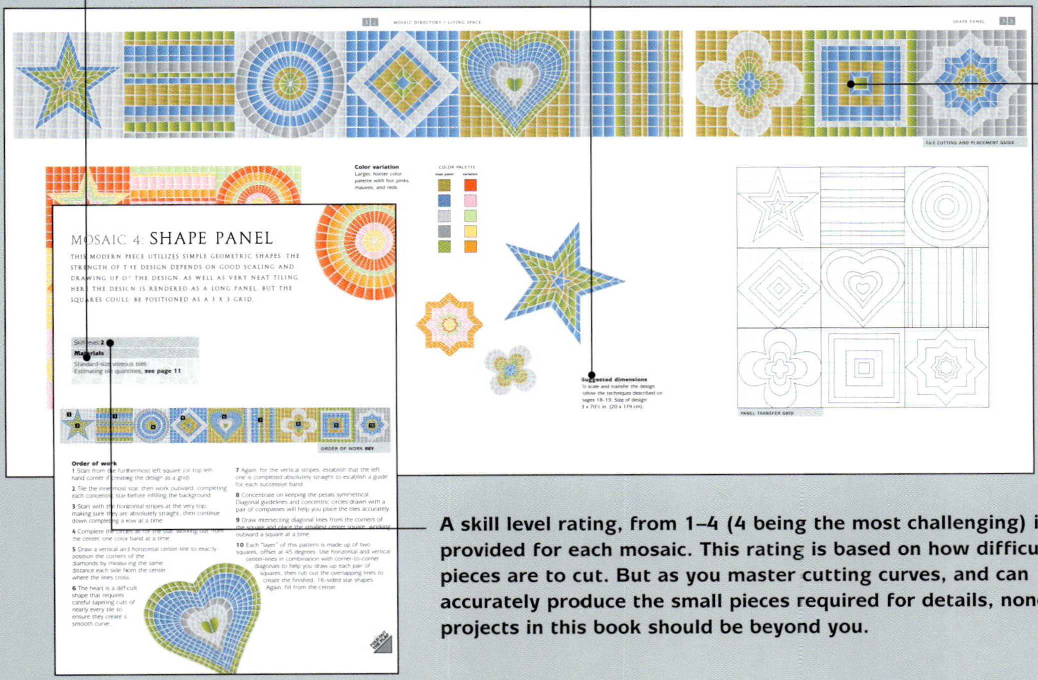

The cutting guide is based around the standard ¾-in. (20-mm) vitreous tiles and every cut and shape has been tested to make sure that the mosaic really can be completed. You'll see how the tiled details and full mosaics in the book exactly match the designs—these are real, workable mosaics.

A skill level rating, from 1–4 (4 being the most challenging) is provided for each mosaic. This rating is based on how difficult the pieces are to cut. But as you master cutting curves, and can accurately produce the small pieces required for details, none of the projects in this book should be beyond you.

TYPES OF TILE

MOST OF THE MURALS IN THIS BOOK CAN BE COMPLETED USING VITREOUS GLASS TILES OR ORDINARY HOUSEHOLD TILES, WHICH ARE COMMONLY AVAILABLE AND RELATIVELY INEXPENSIVE. YOU CAN ALSO COMBINE THESE WITH "FOUND OBJECTS" SUCH AS OLD CROCKERY AND PIECES OF MIRROR GLASS. THE SURFACE OF FINISHED MOSAICS CAN BE EMBELLISHED WITH GLASS BEADS, SEQUINS, AND JEWELRY.

1 Vitreous tiles
These are the "standard" mosaic tiles, made of hard-wearing glass and measuring approximately ⅞ in. (20 mm) square. Available in an almost endless variety of colors and finishes, the undersides are dimpled and beveled to make them easier to fix to surfaces. You can buy these from specialist suppliers or art stores, either loose or on backing sheets.

2 Household tiles
These are the tiles usually used for decorating walls in bathrooms and kitchens. They are available in different sizes but with a more limited color range. The bulk of the tile is made from fired clay, softer than a vitreous tile and therefore easier to cut, shape, and work. The front surface is glazed and smooth.

3 Decorative tiles
Household/ceramic tiles are also available with a variety of patterns which, with careful cutting, you can combine effectively into some mosaic designs.

Estimating tile quantities

You cannot calculate the exact number of tiles a specific mosaic mural will require—wastage will depend on your skill at cutting tiles and the complexity of the design.

As a rule of thumb, work out the area of the finished mural by multiplying its height by its width. Then work out the number of individual tiles that will fit into this area. For example, if the finished piece is to be 39 $\frac{1}{4}$ in. (1 meter) wide by 39 $\frac{1}{4}$ in. (1 meter) tall, and uses $\frac{7}{8}$ in. (20 mm) vitreous tiles, you will need 50 x 50, or 2,500 tiles to fill this area.

However, cutting and shaping tiles will create a lot of waste, perhaps as much as half of this number of tiles. To be on the safe side, order half as much again—i.e. 3,750 tiles in total.

Keep track of how many tiles you use for each project and compare this to the number you ordered. This will allow you to more accurately predict the number of tiles that an individual project is likely to require in the future.

4 "Crocks"
Old plates, crockery, and tiles are available from secondhand and thrift stores. These can be recycled to provide interesting detail within some mosaic designs. However, remember that if you mix these "crocks" with ordinary tiles, there may be variations in thickness that can be difficult to accommodate.

5 Mirrored glass
Mosaic mirror tiles (or pieces of old mirrors) provide eye-catching highlights in a design but can be difficult to work with. Mirrored glass is brittle and prone to shatter when cut. The coating on the underside, which creates the reflection, is also vulnerable to chemical action from glues and grouts.

6 Jewels and sequins
There are numerous tiny sequins, "costume" jewels, and diamantés that you can buy from craft stores to add to the surface of your finished mosaic. However, only embellish a piece in this way after the grout has been allowed to dry for several days. You will also need to find an appropriate glue capable of adhering to the glass surface of the tiles.

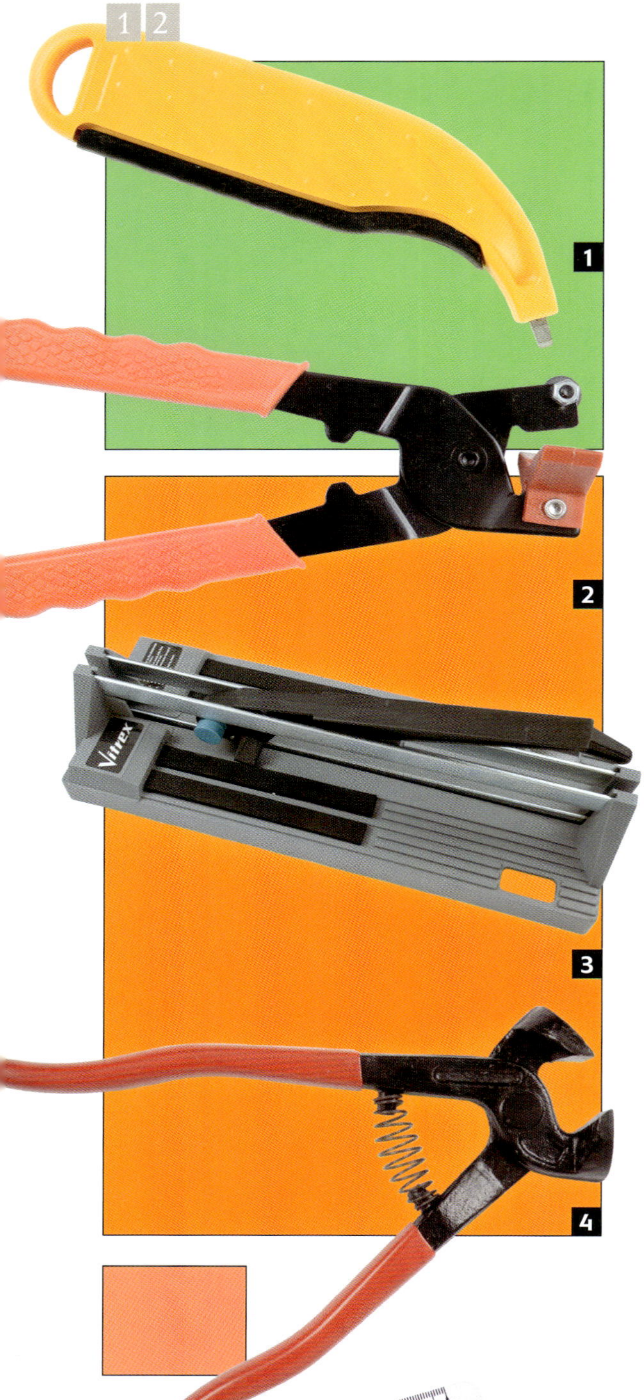

TOOLS AND EQUIPMENT

YOU CAN BEGIN CREATING MOSAICS WITH SOME BASIC TOOLS AND MATERIALS. ASK IN HARDWARE STORES FIRST, AS YOU MAY BE ABLE TO OBTAIN WHAT YOU NEED MORE CHEAPLY THAN FROM SPECIALIST ART SUPPLIERS.

1 Tile scorer
Use this with a steel rule to score the surface of household ceramic tiles.

2 Tile snappers
Place a scored tile into the tile snapper and squeeze slowly to cleanly break the tile in two.

3 Tabletop tile cutter
This is the tool used by professional household tilers—use it only for ceramic tiles (not for vitreous tiles).

4 Nippers
These are the mosaicist's best friend, with which you can cut all types of tile. Look for a solid pair with jaws that align properly. (The spring opens the jaws between cuts so that you can work more quickly with them.)

5 Drawing equipment
You will need pencils, pens, rulers, protractor, compasses, and a ruler to draw up your designs and mark tiles for accurate cutting. (The steel ruler is used with a tile scorer for cutting straight lines on household tiles.)

6 Baseboards
Medium-density fiberboard (MDF) is a stable, strong, and light material on which to create mosaics. A man-made material, it is easy to cut, shape, and drill. An alternative is

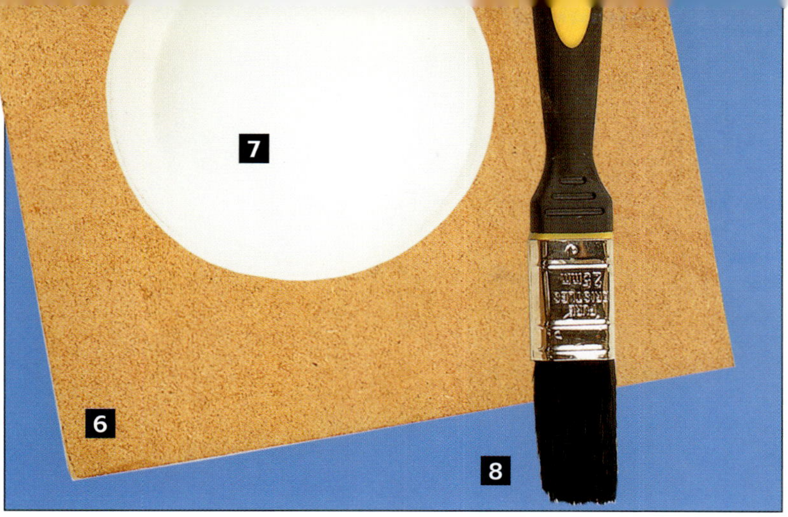

Marine Plywood, which is more resistant to water and therefore better suited to some applications.

7 Glue
To fix tiles to the baseboard a waterproof PVA (Polyvinyl Acetate) glue is best. When wet it is white, but as it sets it turns clear. For outdoor pieces, or if a stronger adhesive than PVA is required, epoxy resin is the answer.

8 Household paintbrush
A paintbrush is useful for applying primer to the baseboard.

9 Grout
Grout is used to fill the gaps between the tiles. It comes as a powder to which you add water and mix, or you can buy ready-to-use in a re-sealable container.

10 Grouting tools
A tiler's squeegee is used to spread and press the grout between the tiles. A sponge is used to clean the surface of the tiles as the grout dries and sets.

11 Safety equipment
Always read the instructions for all the tools and materials that you use, making sure to wear the appropriate safety equipment. Goggles or safety spectacles are essential to prevent fragments injuring your eyes when cutting tiles.

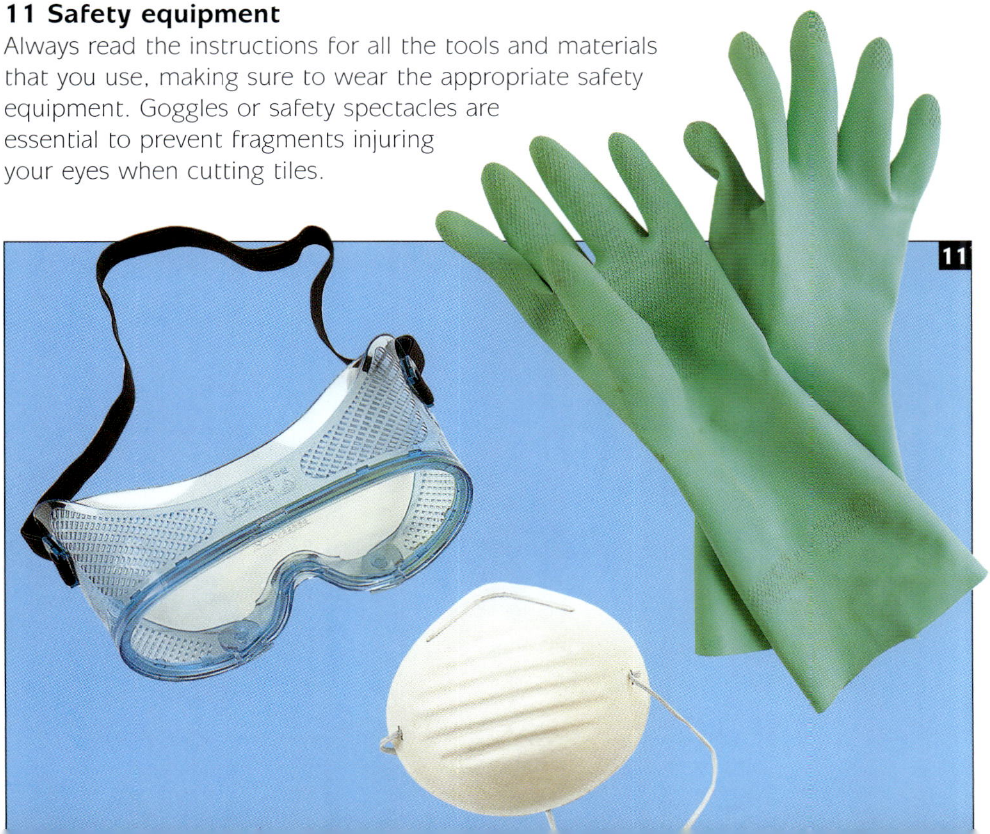

PREPARING SURFACES

MOST OF THE PROJECTS IN THIS BOOK CAN BE CREATED ON MDF RATHER THAN DIRECTLY ONTO A WALL. THIS HAS THE ADVANTAGE OF ALLOWING YOU TO WORK ON A FLAT SURFACE AND FINISH THE MURAL TO YOUR SATISFACTION BEFORE YOU HANG IT.

1 Mark up the board with a pencil and long ruler, making sure that all sides are parallel. (Some craft or hardware stores will cut rectangular boards from larger sheets for a small charge.)

2 MDF can be cut to size with a conventional handsaw.

3 To cut out decorative shapes and curves you can also use an electric jigsaw. Make sure the board is supported properly while cutting it.

4 Thin some PVA glue with water (about half-and-half) to act as a sealant. This will stop the glue from drying out too quickly when sticking tiles onto the board. It will also help stop the board from warping.

5 Apply the diluted PVA with a household paintbrush (rinse this thoroughly in cold water immediately after use).

6 It is a good idea to pre-drill the board with the holes that will be needed to mount it on the wall later. As you tile the design, you can leave out the tiles that would cover these holes, adding them after the mural has been screwed to the wall.

Tips

■ Always cut the baseboard to the correct size before tiling—cutting the board along the edge of a line of tiles that has been glued down is almost impossible. The edge of the board is also a useful guide to keep tiles in straight lines.

■ If cutting with a jigsaw, always wear a face mask because a lot of dust will be created.

■ Use sandpaper to tidy up your saw cuts before you seal the board.

■ The board will be considerably heavier when covered all over with tiles and grout, so make sure you drill sufficient mounting holes—six or, ideally, eight—particularly if hanging a large piece above a bed or valuable piece of furniture.

■ You can also mark up the wall for the screw holes at this stage. Again it is much easier to hold up the board to mark where the holes are needed before it is weighted down with tiles.

Preparation
Preparing the baseboard of the mosaic in advance ensures that the end result is both strong and attractive. By following the steps opposite this finished piece has been securely fastened to the wall but with all the fixings concealed.

CUTTING TILES

BEFORE EMBARKING ON ANY OF THE PROJECTS IN THIS BOOK, PRACTICE USING YOUR TILE NIPPERS UNTIL YOU ARE CONFIDENT THAT YOU CAN ACCURATELY SPLIT AND SHAPE THE TILE PIECES YOU WILL NEED. TILES ARE BRITTLE AND MAY SHATTER–PERSEVERE UNTIL YOU GET IT RIGHT.

Household tiles

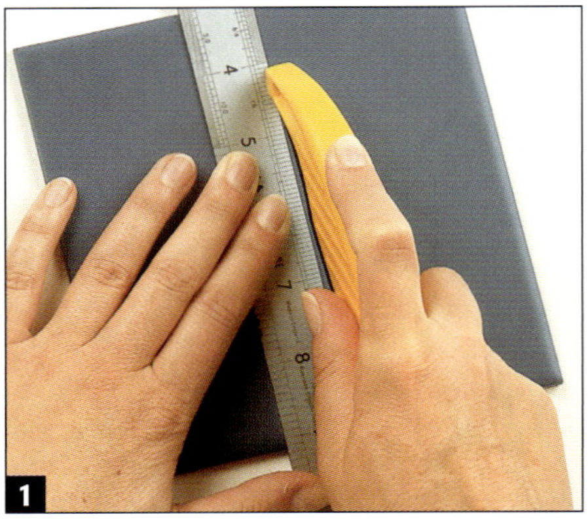

1 You can cut household tiles into regular strips with a tile scorer and snapper.

2 Alternatively a heavy-duty specialist cutter is an easy and accurate way to cut these tiles into thin rectangles.

3 Using the tile nippers, you can then snap each strip into square tiles of the same size.

Vitreous tiles

1 Don't be afraid to draw on the tiles first, with a washable felt-tip pen, so that you can cut each shape accurately.

2 Grip the tile with your fingers, then with the other hand apply firm pressure onto the handles of the nippers, twisting slightly down. The tile will split along the line of the blades of the nipper.

Nibbling
By cutting in from the edge of the tile a bit at a time you can follow the outline of irregular shapes and curves: this technique is known as "nibbling." This works for both household and vitreous tiles.

Cutting circles
Cut circles in both vitreous and household tiles by splitting the tile down to a square close to the size you need, then nibbling along the drawn outline with lots of tiny cuts.

Cutting triangles
Cut diagonally across a square tile to produce two triangular tile pieces. You can halve these again to make even smaller triangles.

Choosing colors

Learning to work with colors and exploiting the rich possibilities that tiles offer are important steps in producing good mosaics. But as well as learning how to be bold with color, you also need to master creating more subtle effects in the way you combine tiles together. No matter how big a collection of tiles you acquire, you will always face some limitations. Unlike a painter, you cannot mix or thin and water down your colors to achieve subtle shades or blends.

Color wheel

The color wheel illustrates some of the important rules of how colors work when placed together. The colors that are near to each other on the wheel are harmonious when placed together, tending to merge rather than clash. Those on opposite sides are known as "complementaries" which, when placed together, will seem almost to react with and separate from each other. You can experiment with tiles from different positions within the color wheel to see the different results.

Tips

warm colors

cool colors

Choose one color palette

Sticking to either warm or cool colors in a piece will give it a strongly atmospheric effect.

Complementary hues

If you have a plain background area to fill, you can avoid boring areas of flat color by mixing different hues, provided that you keep the tones close.

SCALING AND TRANSFERRING

READ THROUGH THIS SECTION A COUPLE OF TIMES SO THAT YOU FULLY UNDERSTAND THE ENLARGEMENT PROCESS–AND CHECK YOUR MATH TO MAKE SURE YOU ARE "BLOWING UP" YOUR DESIGN TO THE SIZE YOU INTEND. SCALING THE DRAWING USING A GRID IS THE TRADITIONAL WAY ARTISTS HAVE PRODUCED LARGE PAINTINGS AND MURALS FOR THOUSANDS OF YEARS. A PHOTOCOPIER MIGHT SEEM THE EASIER WAY TO ACHIEVE THE SAME RESULT, BUT IT CAN ACTUALLY BE MORE WORK TAPING SHEETS OF COPIER PAPER TOGETHER, THAN REACHING FOR A PENCIL AND RULER AND SCALING YOUR DESIGN.

Scaling your drawing

1 Take your original drawing, or better still a photocopy of the drawing, and make a grid of squares over the top using a pencil and ruler. The size of the squares will depend on the size of the drawing—aim for the grid to be between 10 and 15 squares high or wide to cover the drawing. For example, with a drawing 6 in. (15 cm) wide or high, you could most simply draw a grid of 12 x ½ in. squares (1.25 cm).

2 On a large sheet of tracing paper, or thin paper, draw a second grid—the width you want the finished mosaic—with exactly the same number of squares across and down as the one covering the drawing. So, in our example, if you wanted to make the mosaic in. the example above 24 in. (60 cm) across, the grid would need to be four times as wide as the small drawing, meaning that each square of the grid would be 2 in. (5 cm).

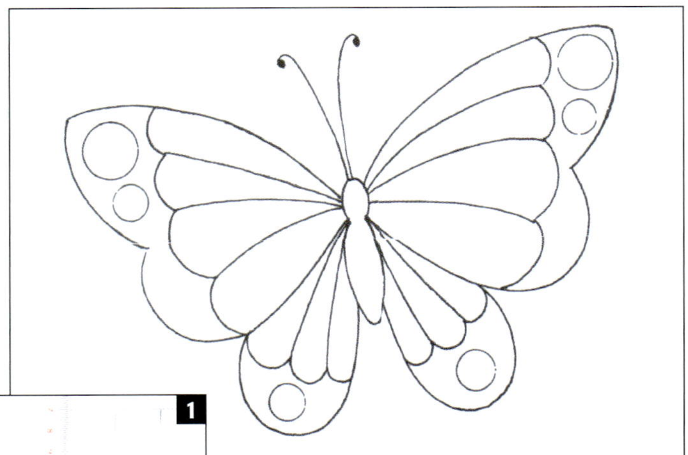

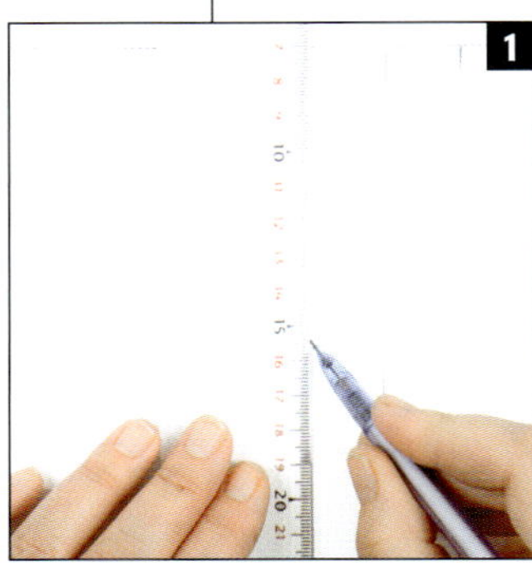

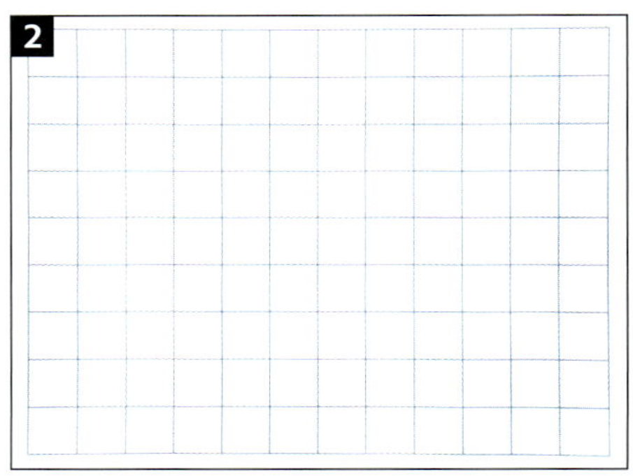

Transferring your drawing

1 Turn your full-sized drawing over and using a soft, thick pencil, go over the back of the drawing, shading along the lines of the design. Use a scribbling motion to transfer lots of pencil onto the paper. (This is easier if you used tracing paper; if not, tape the drawing back-to-front onto a large window to make the paper see-through so that you can follow the lines of the original on the other side.)

1

2 Turn the picture back the right way, tape it in the correct position on the baseboard, then go back over the design, pressing hard so that the soft pencil on the back of the drawing will transfer onto the baseboard. Before removing the drawing, peel it back a corner at a time to check everything has transferred—go over lines you have missed or that are unclear.

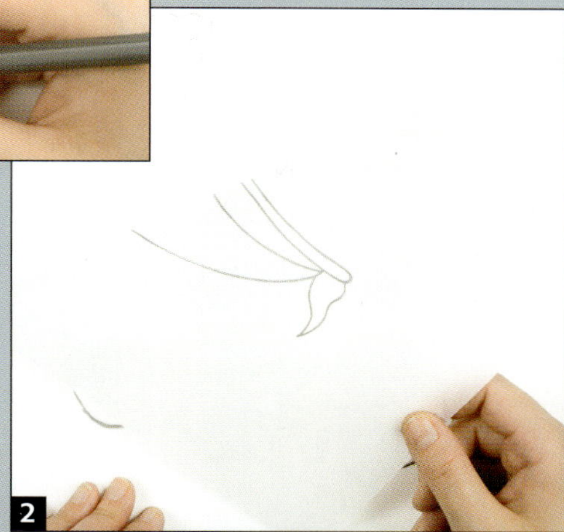
2

3 Now look closely at your small drawing, concentrating on one of the main lines of the design and seeing where it crosses the grid drawn on top. Then mark the same point on your enlarged grid with a dot.

3

4 Follow each line in the small drawing, carefully plotting onto the large grid the path it follows, using the grid as your guide. Use a pencil so you can easily correct any mistakes. When you have plotted as many points as you can, simply join up the dots.

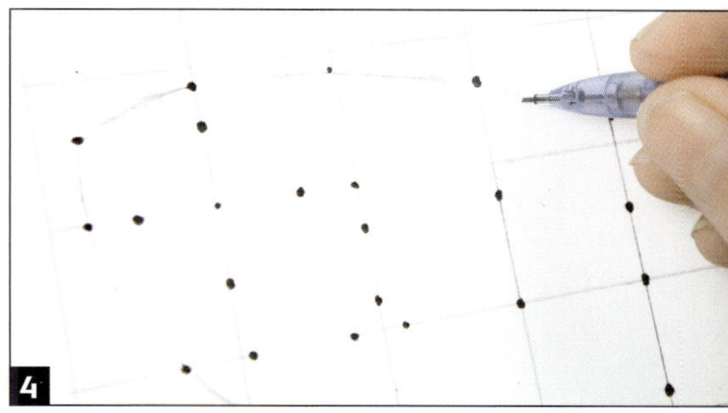
4

5 Check the finished drawing carefully against the "original." Rub out and correct any errors. Persevere to get the drawing right—effort put in now will save frustration later as corrections cannot be made easily to the tiles once they are stuck down.

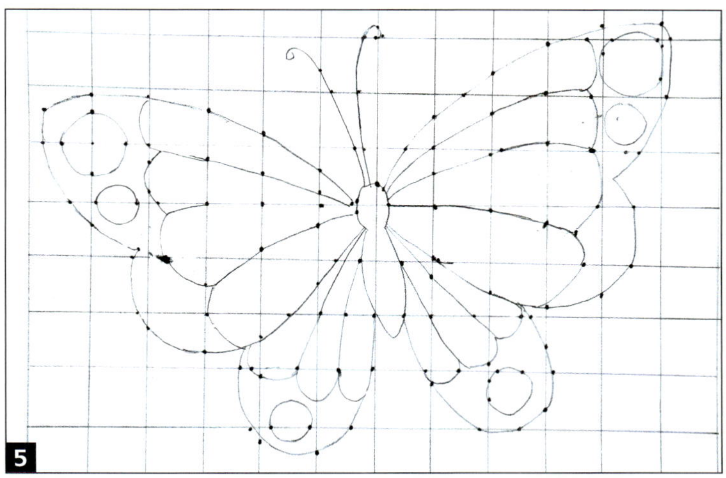
5

PLACING AND GROUTING

MOSAIC TILES MUST BE PLACED AND GLUED SO THAT THEIR SURFACE IS LEVEL. YOU MUST ALSO LEAVE A SMALL BUT EVEN GAP BETWEEN ALL THE TILES TO FILL WITH GROUT. THE GROUT REALLY COMPLETES YOUR MURALS, BRINGING THE TILES TO LIFE. PATIENCE AND PRACTICE ARE REQUIRED TO GET BOTH THESE ELEMENTS RIGHT.

Placing tiles evenly
Whatever the size of your tiles, make sure that the space between them is even. It must not be too far apart, otherwise the tiles will appear to be sinking in a quicksand of grout. However, they must not be too close or there will not be sufficient space for the grout. In time, you will learn what is pleasing and looks right. At first, simply enjoy experimenting and learning how different spacings look.

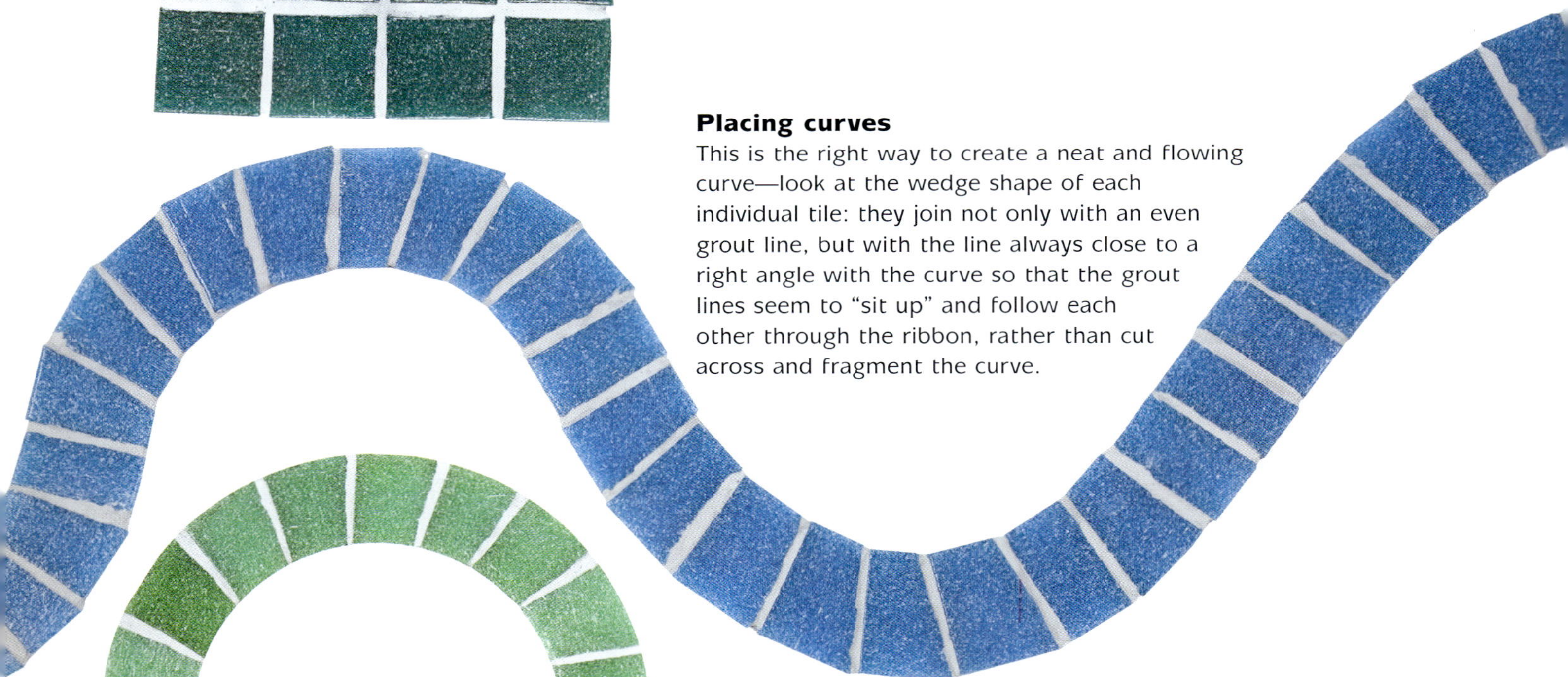

Placing curves
This is the right way to create a neat and flowing curve—look at the wedge shape of each individual tile: they join not only with an even grout line, but with the line always close to a right angle with the curve so that the grout lines seem to "sit up" and follow each other through the ribbon, rather than cut across and fragment the curve.

Placing circles
The tiles have been cut to create the outline of a circle—each tile is evenly cut, of similar size, with the edges angled so that they "fit" in an even way. The end result is a strong but harmonious shape.

Gluing details
For detailed areas, work on a small area at a time. Cut your tiles and position them over the drawn design to make sure everything "fits." Only when you are happy, stick them down a piece at a time, applying a small blob of glue to the back of the tile with a fine brush.

Gluing large areas
When gluing down a large area with a simple fill, you can use a brush or spatula to apply glue liberally to the area of the baseboard you wish to cover. Quickly press your pre-cut tiles into the glue, sliding them if necessary so that they are accurately positioned. However, only spread glue over an area that you can tile in five or ten minutes before it dries.

Grouting

1 Adding color: most bought grout is white. While this is fine for domestic tiling, it looks far too bright when used on a mosaic. Add acrylic or poster paints to white grout to tone it down, using colors that complement your design, or, if in doubt, go for a light gray by adding black.

2 Applying grout: leave the piece at least overnight to ensure that the glue is totally dry before grouting. Spoon a large blob of mixed and colored grout onto the surface of the mosaic. With a squeegee spread and press the grout over and in between the tiles using firm pressure. When all the gaps are filled, use the squeegee to clean off any excess.

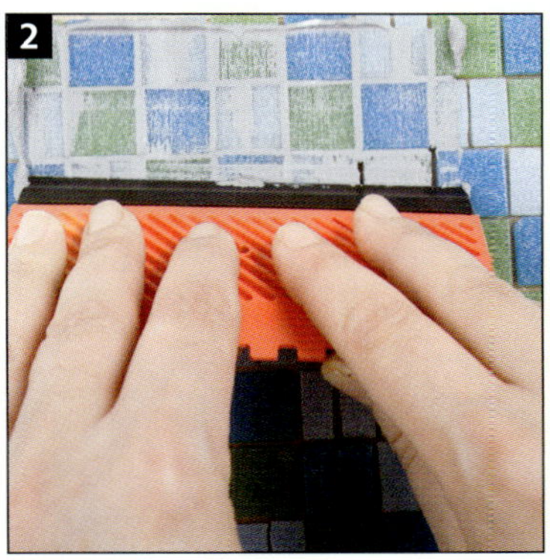

3 Let the grout partially dry, then wipe over with a damp (not soaking) sponge or cloth to remove grout from the surface of the tiles. Use firm, sweeping strokes—don't fuss too much or you risk disturbing the grout from between the tiles.

MOUNTING AND FINISHING

THE FINISHED AND GROUTED MOSAIC PIECE WILL BE VERY HEAVY COMPARED TO AN ORDINARY PICTURE, SO IT IS IMPORTANT THAT YOU SECURE IT PROPERLY TO THE WALL. PERMANENT FIXING INVOLVES HIDING THE MOUNTINGS UNDERNEATH TILES. ALTERNATIVELY, YOU CAN USE "KEYHOLE" FIXTURES, WHICH MAKE REMOVING AND RE-HANGING THE PIECE EASIER AT A LATER DATE.

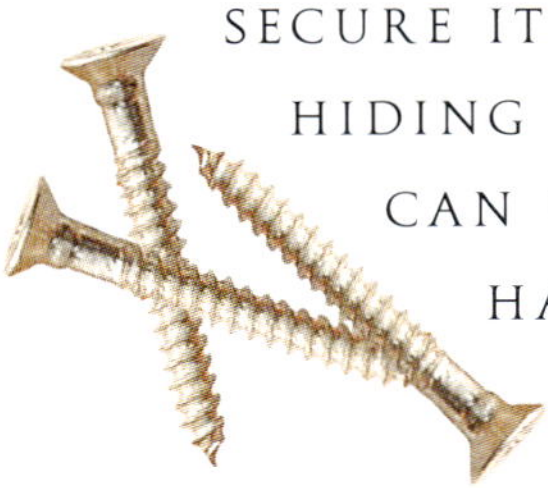

Permanent fixture

1 If you followed the guidance in the section "Preparing surfaces" (see page 14) to pre-drill the board prior to tiling, you simply need to find someone to help hold the mosaic up while you mark the wall with the position of the screw holes you made in the board. Use a level to get everything straight; mark the holes, then drill these and put in the appropriate wall plug to hold the screws. Use good, solid screws, at least 1 in. (25 mm) long, in 8 or 10 gauge.

2 Once your mural is on the wall, glue down the missing tile pieces to cover the screw heads.

3 When the glue has set, grout the tiles you have added exactly as you grouted the main area of the mural. Well done if you saved a bit of mixed and colored grout to ensure a perfect match.

4 Leave this grout to go hard for a couple of days, then have a final clean up with warm water and a sponge/scourer to leave the tiles really gleaming. If you want, you can add a simple frame to the mural by tacking thin strips of wood to the edge of the baseboard to conceal both the board and the edge of the tiles.

Removable fixture
Alternatively, you can fix the finished mural to the wall using keyhole fittings from an hardware store. These are generally brass fittings that screw to the back of the board. Use short screws so that you don't screw right through the baseboard and dislodge the tiles. You should use as many as eight fittings for large, heavy pieces.

Indirect method

All the designs in this book can be easily created using what is known as the "direct" method—that is cutting and gluing the tile pieces directly onto the baseboard. It is a quick and easy way to work, and you can immediately see the results. It is probably the best way for beginners to start working in mosaics.

However, sometimes it is not possible to work on a mosaic in its final "site." In this case the "indirect" method is used, where the tiles are placed upside-down on an adhesive backing sheet, then transferred later to a floor, wall, or other surface. This method only works with vitreous glass tiles—household ceramic tiles have the same clay back which means it is impossible to keep track of colors and the design as you work.

1 The design or drawing is transferred, in reverse, onto a brown paper backing sheet. The pieces are cut and laid face down onto the drawing, and glued in place with a water-soluble glue. The finished mosaic is allowed to set.

2 The sheet (or sheets in the case of a big project) is then taken to its final site taking care not to dislodge any tiles. The area where it is to be laid is thoroughly covered with a thick layer of waterproof tile adhesive. The mosaic sheet is then pressed face down into this adhesive—in other words with the brown paper backing facing up. A board or slab of flat wood can be used to make sure the tiles are level.

3 The adhesive is allowed to dry thoroughly, then the backing sheet is soaked and removed to reveal the design beneath. Grouting and finishing proceeds exactly as for the "direct" method.

MOSAIC DIRECTORY

The following pages contain 50 unique mural designs for you to copy, adapt, and enjoy. If you have worked through the techniques section and practiced cutting and laying tiles, then you are ready to go. It is probably best to start with one of the simple pieces in order to develop your skills, patience, and accuracy before moving on to the more ambitious pieces. Refer to the skill level rating on each page to understand how easy or challenging each piece will be to complete.

MOSAIC 1: HARBOR BOATS

THIS NATURALISTIC, PEACEFUL SCENE, EVOCATIVE OF SEASIDE HOLIDAYS, WOULD HAVE A CALMING EFFECT IN ALMOST ANY ROOM. THE DESIGN HAS BEEN RENDERED IN CERAMIC TILES SO THAT THE PLANKS OF THE BOATS' HULLS CAN BE CUT FROM SINGLE, LARGE PIECES.

Skill level: **2**

Materials

Standard-size vitreous tiles
Estimating tile quantities, **see page 11**

VARIATION: PASTELS

Color variation
As an alternative to natural, earthy browns and blues try a softer, bleached-out set of pastel colors to give the effect of an old, hand-tinted photograph.

Order of work

1 Begin with the anchor in the foreground which is a point of focus. Make it appear embedded in the sand rather than floating in space.

2 Move on to the first boat, beginning with the portholes, then do the central band that runs around the hull. The windows in the deckhouse of the boat are cut as single, large chunks of tile.

3 Now tile the gulls in the foreground: start with the details of the eyes and beaks, then move downward filling the bodies, and outward to create the wings.

4 Follow the same order for the second boat as for the first.

5 Complete the stones on the beach then the large, sandy areas, following the fill shown in the illustration to give a sense of perspective.

6 The sea can be filled haphazardly, mixing areas of blue and white, but cut the tiles along the edge carefully to create the fullness of the waves breaking on the shore.

7 Begin the harbor wall by carefully dovetailing the circles of the life buoys.

8 Fill in the rows of stone blocks: cut these as simple rectangles but then nibble the corners to give a rounded, uneven effect like real stones.

9 Another seagull: follow the order of tiling as before.

10–14 Work through the houses in order from foreground to background. Begin each with the window and door detail, then complete the walls with large tile pieces. The roofs can be made from long strips of tile laid parallel. Some of the walls of the houses can be made in the same way to suggest painted weatherboards.

15 Make the circling gulls from slivers of tile.

16 Cut rounded, billowing tiles for the clouds.

17 Finish with a simple, plain fill for the background sky.

ORDER OF WORK **KEY**

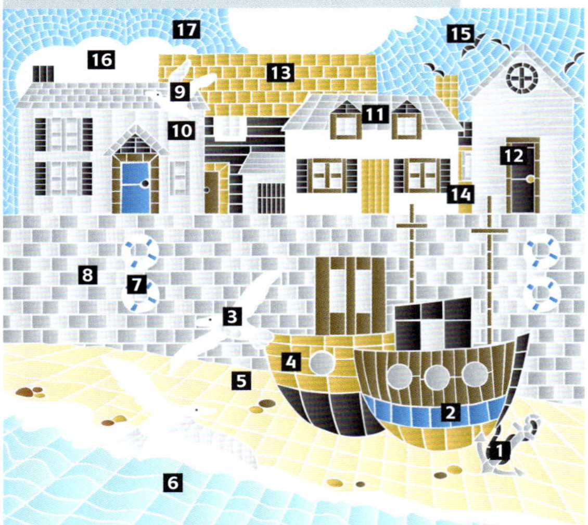

TILE CUTTING AND PLACEMENT GUIDE

COLOR PALETTE

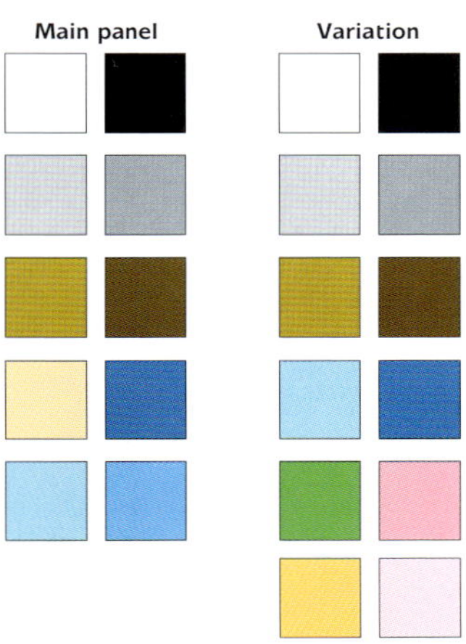

PANEL TRANSFER GRID

Suggested dimensions

To scale and transfer the design follow the techniques described on pages 18–19. Size of design: 23¼ x 21¼ in. (59 x 54 cm).

MOSAIC 2: TATTOOED HEART

BASED ON AN OLD-FASHIONED TATTOO, THE CENTRAL "SASH" RUNNING ACROSS THE HEART WOULD NORMALLY FEATURE THE NAME OF A LOVED ONE OR A MOTTO. YOU CAN ADAPT THE DESIGN TO INCLUDE A NAME, MESSAGE, OR SLOGAN. THIS COLOR VARIATION USES THE TRADITIONAL RED AND BLUE OF THE TATTOOIST'S INK.

Skill level: **2**

Materials

Standard-size vitreous tiles
Estimating tile quantities, **see page 11**

ORDER OF WORK **KEY**

COLOR PALETTE

Main panel | Variation

VARIATION: DARK AND DRAMATIC

Order of work

1 Begin with the sash: either start with the dots, or, if you are going to include a motto, draw up and then tile the lettering.

2 Next complete the red center panel of the heart and then the surrounding trim, placing the dark "dashes" of tile first.

3 Now for the center of the flowers. Cut splinters of tile to give the sharp, pointed effect of their petals.

4 Next tile the surrounding doves.

5 Move on to the stars.

6 Finish with a simple, flat fill for the background.

Color variation

A darker, more dramatic background is used in this version, with a warm yellow accentuating the flowers. The heart, however, remains blood red.

TILE CUTTING AND PLACEMENT GUIDE

Suggested dimensions

To scale and transfer the design follow the techniques described on pages 18–19. Size of design: 37½ x 23¼ in. (95 x 59 cm).

PANEL TRANSFER GRID

MOSAIC 3: STAN AND OLLIE

A PORTRAIT OF THE BELOVED COMEDY DUO, WHICH CAPTURES THE GENTLE WARMTH OF THEIR HUMOR. IT MAY APPEAR DAUNTING, BUT THE DESIGN USES JUST THREE COLOR TONES, AND PROVIDING YOU TAKE GREAT CARE WITH THE CRUCIAL DETAILS OF THE EYES AND MOUTHS YOU WILL BE ABLE TO CREATE THIS "PHOTO-REALIST" EFFECT.

Skill level: **3**

Materials

Standard-size vitreous tiles
Estimating tile quantities, **see page 11**

ORDER OF WORK **KEY**

Order of work

1 Begin with the pale/highlight areas of the faces.

2 Move on to the mid-tones: follow the outlines of the design as accurately as possible, nibbling at tiles to create accurate, soft curves.

3 Complete the dark areas. Although the design is flat, you can suggest the form of the hats and figures by using the flow of the fill to give shape.

4 Finish with the background as either a flat-fill or contouring around the figures.

Color variation

Warm brown and ocher tones give a sepia effect to this version.

VARIATION: SEPIA

PANEL TRANSFER GRID

COLOR PALETTE

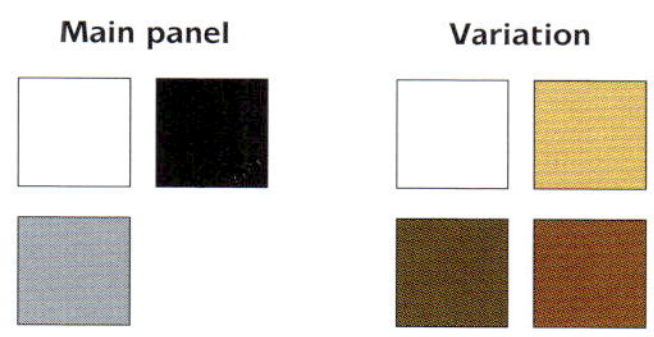

Suggested dimensions

To scale and transfer the design follow the techniques described on pages 18–19. Size of design: 23¼ x 28½ in. (59 x 72 cm).

TILE CUTTING AND PLACEMENT GUIDE

Color variation
Hotter color palette with hot pinks, mauves, and reds.

COLOR PALETTE

Main panel **Variation**

Suggested dimensions
To scale and transfer the design follow the techniques described on pages 18–19. Size of design: 8 x 70½ in. (20 x 179 cm).

TILE CUTTING AND PLACEMENT GUIDE

PANEL TRANSFER GRID

MOSAIC 5: RETRO ROSES

THIS STYLIZED DESIGN HAS A 1950S LOOK. THE ROSE PETALS ARE SIMPLIFIED LIKE A STENCIL DESIGN, AND THE WHOLE PALETTE REQUIRES JUST SIX DIFFERENT COLORS.

Skill level: **4**

Materials

Standard-size vitreous tiles
Estimating tile quantities, **see page 11**

Order of work

1 Depending on the size, you can cut each of the polka dot circles on the vase from a single tile. A crackle fill around the circles will give a more 1950s feel and avoids the problem of following the shape of the vase that a regular fill demands.

2 Begin the smaller of the roses by completing the darker-toned areas first, keeping the curves smooth by using small cuts

3 Complete the lighter-toned areas of the petals.

4 This smaller bud follows the same order as the flowers.

5 Do the same for the larger flower: the darker tones first, then the light areas. Then tile the stalks in a dark tone.

6 The leaves are abstracted with a simple outline. A symmetrical fill will suggest the vein of the leaf.

7 Complete the stripes of the background wallpaper—keep them even in thickness and spacing.

8 Use a regular, rectangular fill for the rest of the wallpaper.

ORDER OF WORK **KEY**

PANEL TRANSFER GRID

Suggested dimensions

To scale and transfer the design follow the techniques described on pages 18–19.
Size of design: 22 x 10¼ in. (56 x 26 cm).

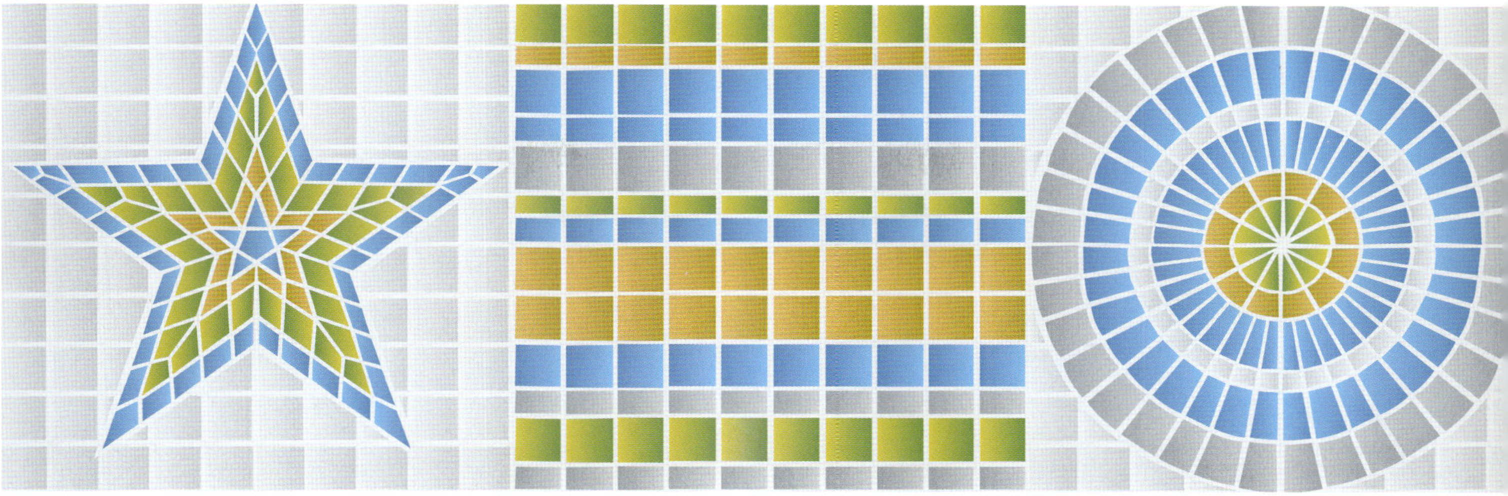

VARIATION: HOT

MOSAIC 4: SHAPE PANEL

THIS MODERN PIECE UTILIZES SIMPLE GEOMETRIC SHAPES. THE STRENGTH OF THE DESIGN DEPENDS ON GOOD SCALING AND DRAWING UP OF THE DESIGN, AS WELL AS VERY NEAT TILING. HERE THE DESIGN IS RENDERED AS A LONG PANEL, BUT THE SQUARES COULD BE POSITIONED AS A 3 X 3 GRID.

Skill level: **2**

Materials

Standard-size vitreous tiles
Estimating tile quantities, **see page 11**

ORDER OF WORK **KEY**

Order of work

1 Start from the furthermost left square (or top left-hand corner if creating the design as a grid).

2 Tile the innermost star, then work outward, completing each concentric star before infilling the background.

3 Start with the horizontal stripes at the very top, making sure they are absolutely straight, then continue down completing a row at a time.

4 Complete the circles as for the star, working out from the center, one color band at a time.

5 Draw a vertical and horizontal center-line to exactly position the corners of the diamonds by measuring the same distance each side from the center where the lines cross.

6 The heart is a difficult shape that requires careful tapering cuts of nearly every tile to ensure they create a smooth curve.

7 Again, for the vertical stripes, establish that the left one is completed absolutely straight to establish a guide for each successive band.

8 Concentrate on keeping the petals symmetrical. Diagonal guidelines and concentric circles drawn with a pair of compasses will help you place the tiles accurately.

9 Draw intersecting diagonal lines from the corners of the square and place the smallest center square, working outward a square at a time

10 Each "layer" of this pattern is made up of two squares, offset at 45 degrees. Use horizontal and vertical center-lines in combination with corner-to-corner diagonals to help you draw up each pair of squares, then rub out the overlapping lines to create the finished, 16-sided star shapes. Again, fill from the center.

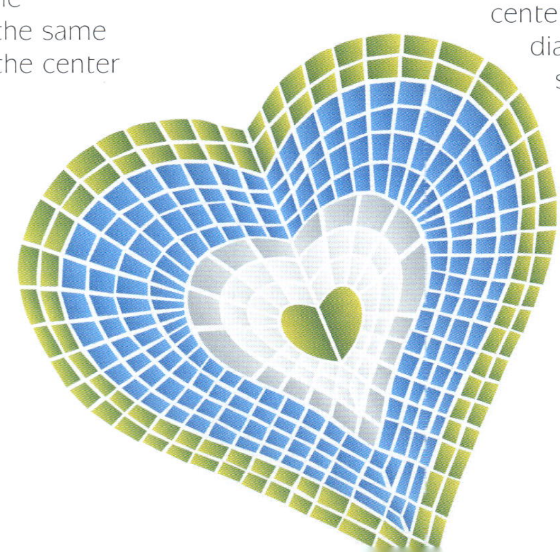

FOLD OUT THE FLAP

TILE CUTTING AND PLACEMENT GUIDE

COLOR PALETTE

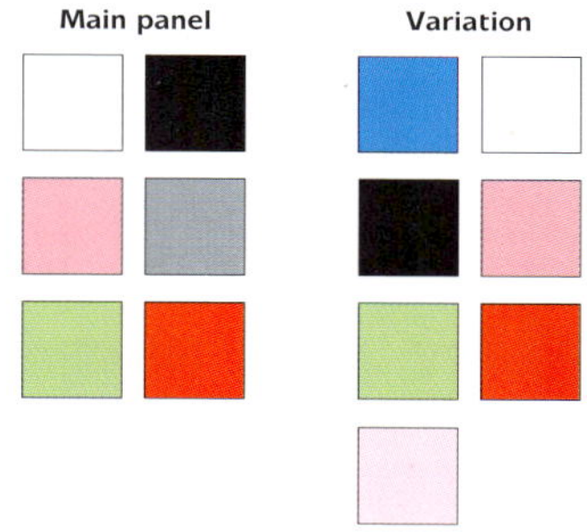

VARIATION: GARISH

Color variation

This version uses a garish blue, with one of the roses in a complementary pink shade.

MOSAIC 6: DOLL'S HOUSE

THIS HOMELY DOLL'S HOUSE SUGGESTS THE OLD HOUSES FOUND IN NEW ENGLAND. YOU COULD PERSONALIZE IT TO MATCH ELEMENTS OF YOUR OWN HOME: THE NUMBER ON THE DOOR, THE EXTERIOR COLOR, OR DRAPES. THE WEATHERBOARD EFFECT IS ACHIEVED BY USING STRIPS OF TILES. YOU COULD ALSO GIVE THE PICTURE A "WINTRY" FEEL BY COVERING THE ROOF IN SNOW AND PLACING HOLLY ON THE DOOR TO MAKE A CENTERPIECE FOR YOUR CHRISTMAS DECORATIONS.

VARIATION: WARM PALETTE

Color variation
This variation uses a warmer palette, with beige details.

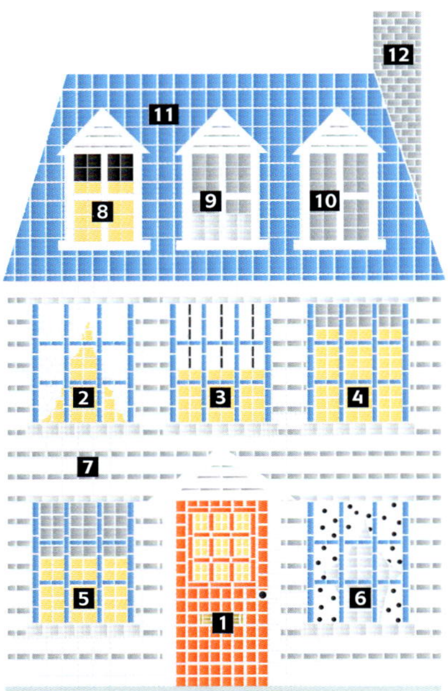

ORDER OF WORK **KEY**

Skill level: **3**

Materials

Standard-size vitreous tiles, Estimating title quantities, **see page 11**

Order of work

1 Begin the door with the details of the letterbox and door handle. You could simplify the door, placing your own house number within the rectangular space instead.

2–6 For all the windows begin with the frame then the sill, then move on to the drapes where you can introduce any variety of patterns and designs.

7 The weatherboarding is emphasized by narrower bands of darker tiles, cut neatly and carefully to get the feeling of straight, ruled lines.

8–10 The upper windows follow the previous order with the addition of the small gables above.

11 For the roof, start from the ridge, working down. Make this very simple by using a rectangular fill, then work outward to create the angled edges. For more naturalistic looking tiles, you will need to draw up receding lines for all the tiles which will involve a large number of very accurate cuts.

12 Finish off with the tiles for the chimney, offsetting small rectangular tiles in alternating rows exactly as a bricklayer would.

PANEL TRANSFER GRID

COLOR PALETTE

Main panel Variation

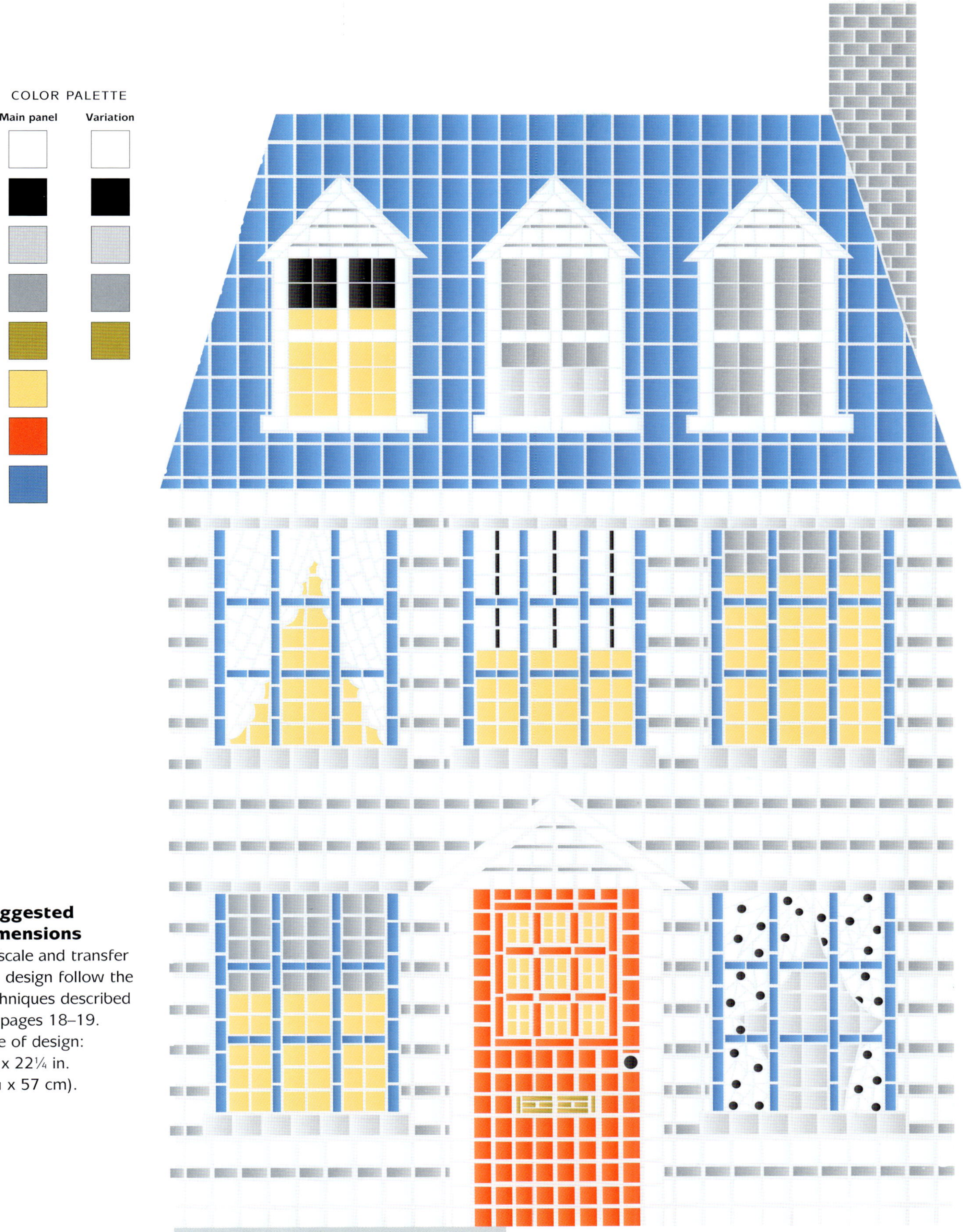

Suggested dimensions

To scale and transfer the design follow the techniques described on pages 18–19. Size of design: 37 x 22¼ in. (94 x 57 cm).

TILE CUTTING AND PLACEMENT GUIDE

MOSAIC 7: MASK

THIS DESIGN IS BASED ON A SMALL PAPIER-MÂCHÉ MASK FROM THE ASHMOLEAN MUSEUM IN OXFORD, ENGLAND. THE FIRST COLOR VARIATION IS VERY CLOSE TO THE ORIGINAL COLORS. THE DESIGN WORKS BEST IF YOU CUT THE BASEBOARD TO THE OUTLINE OF THE MASK, OTHERWISE SURROUND THE MASK WITH A WHITE OR NEUTRAL BACKGROUND.

Skill level: **2**

Materials

Standard-size vitreous tiles, glass costume "jewels," *bindis* (the ornamental mark worn by Hindu women on their foreheads)
Estimating title quantities, **see page 11**

Order of work

1 Begin with the eyes, trying to create as near perfect a circle as possible to give a staring look. The white of the eye is created using two triangles of tile, with a concave curve cut to fit around the iris. The rim is cut with small tiles. The "dots" are made with small circles of tiles to which you could glue glass jewels or sequins after grouting.

2 To create the nose; cut and lay the tiles for the nostrils first, then tile upward, tapering the line to a fine point; keep the curve of the line as smooth as possible.

3 Next, tile the mouth and the mustache taking care to get the shape of the tight, curled ends.

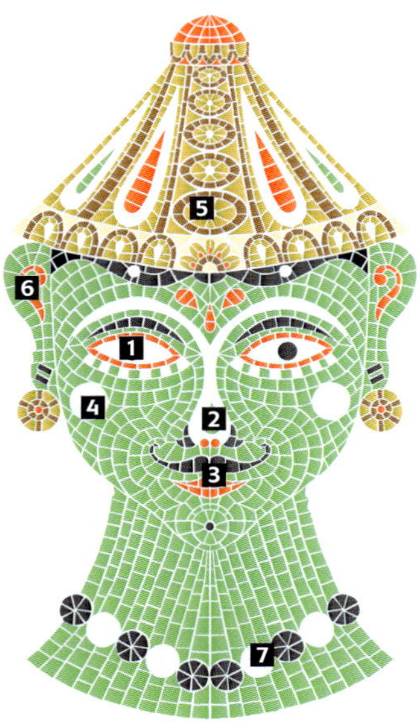

ORDER OF WORK **KEY**

4 Place the dimple on the chin, the markings on the forehead, and the shapes on the cheeks, then the hairline and eyebrows. Fill the face with a contoured fill that winds around the facial details.

5 Move on to the hat, starting with the smallest details then working outward. Work to ensure the symmetry of the design, establishing the central band first.

6 Now complete the inner shape of the ear and the earring before infilling the whole shape.

7 The necklace is completed next—the beads are too big to cut from a single tile, so use triangular cuts and place these like slices of a tiny pie.

VARIATION: COOL PALETTE

Color variation

This blue-colored version is slightly cooler—it could be decorated with jewels or a *bindi*.

PANEL TRANSFER GRID

Suggested dimensions

To scale and transfer the design follow the techniques described on pages 18–19. Size of design: 23¼ x 16½ in. (59 x 42 cm).

COLOR PALETTE

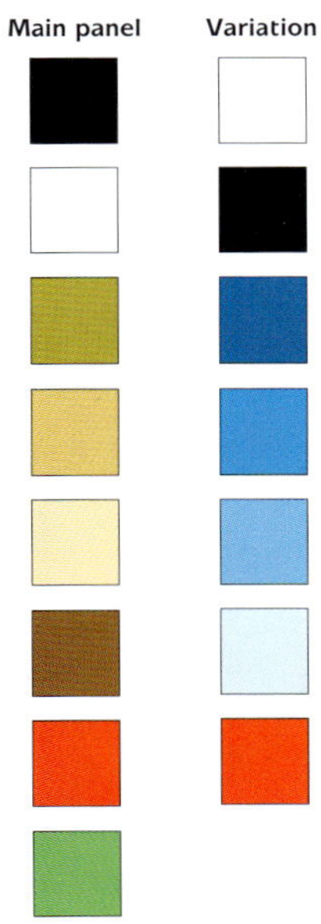

TILE CUTTING AND PLACEMENT GUIDE

MOSAIC 8: FEMME FATALE

THIS SUMPTUOUS, DECADENT PIECE HAS A HOST OF PATTERNS AND COLORS FRAMING THE CENTRAL, MESMERIZING FIGURE WHO APPEARS LIKE SOME FILM STAR OF THE SILENT SCREEN. THE LUSCIOUS MIXTURE OF REDS AND PINKS ALMOST SEEMS TO CARRY THE HEAVY SCENT OF ROSES.

Skill level: **3**

Materials

Standard-size vitreous tiles
Estimating tile quantities, **see page 11**

Order of work

1 The few pieces of tile that make the eyebrows, lips, and eyes are vital to establish the shape of the face and are the center around which the whole picture works. Persevere until you have cut the pieces exactly and discard any that are even slightly imperfect, or you may regret it later. Fill the face following the contours of the eyes and cheekbones. You can attempt some very light shadowing if you have any subtle, off-white tiles.

PANEL TRANSFER GRID

Suggested dimensions

To scale and transfer the design follow the techniques described on pages 18–19.
Size of design: $28\frac{3}{4} \times 21\frac{7}{8}$ in. (73 x 55.5 cm).

ORDER OF WORK **KEY**

2 Place the flower in the hair. (When the piece is complete and grouted, you could embellish this with diamanté stones.)

3 Do the streaks in the hair first, then the mass of the hair.

4 Next, place the jewelry. Add highlights, if you wish, on the bracelet and rings.

5 As with the face, the arms, shoulders, and hands should be contour-filled to enhance their shape. Persevere with the hands in particular to ensure that they are sufficiently delicate. Bright red nails will help to elongate the fingers.

6 The polka dots are next; then surround these with the main color of the dress.

7 Place the central circle of the earrings then surround each with petal-shaped tiles.

8 The zebra print is quite tight to fit together; start with the black tiles, then fill in between.

9 For the flowers work outward; the concentric shapes of the petals gradually increase in size.

10 The background should be filled in with evenly sized and equally spaced pieces of tile.

11 Split tiles into long rectangles and place these carefully to create a thin, inner border.

12 Lay the semicircles of the outer border next, then the triangular pointed "caps." Squeeze more petals into the gaps in between and fill in the spaces that are left with small fragments of tile.

VARIATION: SEPIA PHOTOGRAPH

Color variation

This sepia-color palette gives the sense of an old photograph, but the character still maintains her smouldering sultriness.

TILE CUTTING AND PLACEMENT GUIDE

COLOR PALETTE

Main panel **Variation**

MOSAIC 9: TREE OF LIFE

THIS PIECE WAS INSPIRED BY THE WORK OF THE AUSTRIAN ARTIST GUSTAV KLIMT. IF YOU CAN AFFORD GOLD TILES THEN YOU COULD EMULATE THE RICH, GOLD ORNAMENTATION OF THE ORIGINAL. IF NOT, THIS INTERPRETATION IS JUST AS DRAMATIC– THE STRONG, BLACK BACKGROUND HELPS HOLD AND DEFINE THE COMPLEX, TENDRIL-LIKE DESIGN.

Skill level: **4**

Materials

Standard-size vitreous tiles
Estimating tile quanities, **see page 11**

Color variation
This version utilizes a softer pink to provide the framing color to the birds. As in the first example, using the same color palette for each bird establishes a visual path for the eye to follow through the picture.

PANEL TRANSFER GRID

VARIATION: SOFTER

COLOR PALETTE

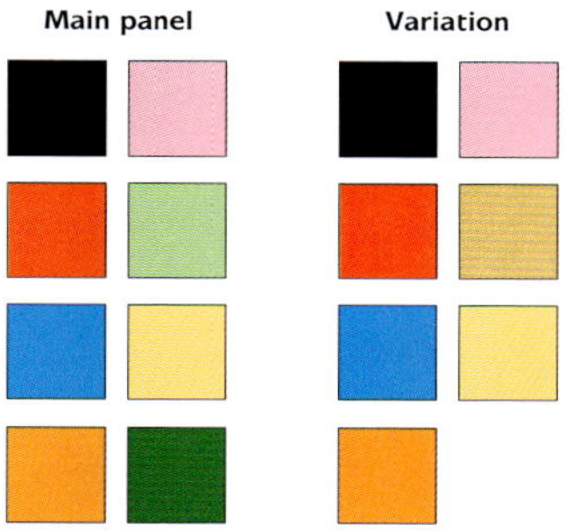

Suggested dimensions

To scale and transfer the design follow the techniques described on pages 18–19. Size of design: 41¼ x 31¾ in. (105 x 80.5cm).

ORDER OF WORK **KEY**

TILE CUTTING AND PLACEMENT GUIDE

Order of work

1 Begin with the heart of the tree, carefully cutting the tiles to give a neat outline to both the inner and outer areas of color.

2 Now do the bodies of each of the birds, placing the eyes and two triangles of the beaks first.

3 Add the tails and wings to the bodies, fanning outward, completing each band of color one after another.

4 Now place all the leaves. Each leaf is made up of two tones of color, so work down the design completing one half first, working from the center line of the leaf, before doing the mirror image in the second color.

5 The trunk and branches are tricky as the fill should have a continuous, curvaceous look but, at the same time, you need to work around the shapes of the birds and leaves.

6 Finish off the background. Again, try and follow the shape of the trees to accentuate the curves of the design, patiently cutting around the foreground detail.

MOSAIC 10: BLOOMING FLOWERS

THIS TRADITIONAL STILL LIFE DESIGN IS BURSTING WITH COLORS AND SHAPES. AN ABUNDANCE OF FLOWERS SPILLS TO THE GROUND AND INTO THE PATTERN OF THE VASE ITSELF.

Skill level: **2**

Materials

Standard-size vitreous tiles or household ceramic tiles
Estimating tile quantities, **see page 11**

PANEL TRANSFER GRID

Suggested dimensions
To scale and transfer the design follow the techniques described on pages 18–19. Size of design: 24¾ x 13⅜ in. (63 x 34 cm).

ORDER OF WORK **KEY**

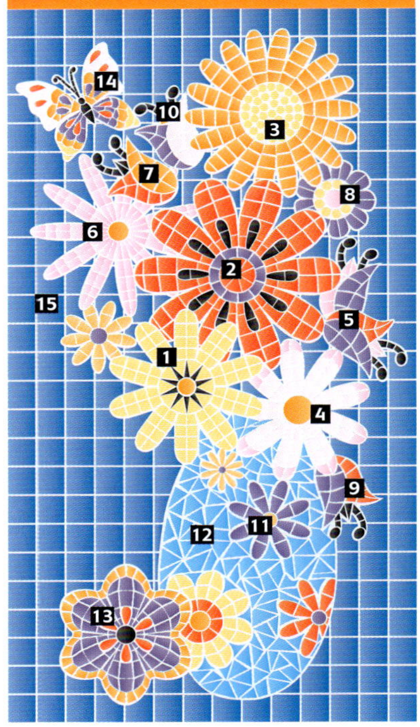

Order of work

1–10 Follow the same process for all the flowers. Begin with those in the front of the picture—those that mask other flowers that are behind them. Always work from the center outward, keeping the radial fills even and balanced around the centers. The small circles and stamens require little cuts and careful placement.

11–12 The flowers on the vase work in the same way, and are then surrounded by a crackle fill to create the body of the vase.

13 Place the flower on the floor.

14 Begin the butterfly with the body and then place the patterns of the wing; cutting the pieces for each wing to match its opposite number. Fill the surrounding areas of the wings and then place the antennae, cutting tiny shards of tile for these.

15 To make the background easier the spaces between the flower petals are filled first with smaller pieces of tile. The bulk of the background is then laid as a simple grid in the same color.

VARIATION: DARKER TONES

Color variation

This variation is just as bright as the main one, but with a darker set of tones, and the background providing more weight.

COLOR PALETTE

Main panel **Variation**

TILE CUTTING AND PLACEMENT GUIDE

MOSAIC 11: BUTTERFLIES

THESE BUTTERFLIES COULD BE PLACED TOGETHER IN A FRAMED BACKGROUND ON A WALL, OR ALTERNATIVELY, TILED ONTO BASEBOARDS CUT OUT TO THEIR OUTLINE USING A JIGSAW. THIS WOULD CREATE THREE SEPARATE BUTTERFLIES, WHICH COULD BE POSITIONED WHEREVER YOU LIKE. THIS PIECE CALLS FOR BRIGHT, PRETTY COLORS, WHICH YOU COULD KEEP VERY SIMPLIFIED, OR YOU COULD WORK FROM PICTURES OF REAL BUTTERFLIES, REPRODUCING THE WONDERFUL ABSTRACT DESIGNS OF NATURE.

Skill level: **2**

Materials

Standard-size vitreous tiles
Estimating tile quantities, **see page 11**

Order of work

1 First butterfly: begin with the main body of the butterfly. If producing these as cut-outs do not attempt antennae as they would be too fragile, but you can include these using tiny, contrasting tones if a background surrounds them.

2 Then move to the wings. Each butterfly is symmetrical, so that you can scale up your drawing of the body and one wing—ideally on to tracing paper—transfer one wing to your baseboard, then turn over the tracing and "rub down" the wing on the other side. Begin tiling the smallest details—the center of the flowers—then work your way out, completing the flower detail a color band at a time.

3 The backfill follows the shapes of the flowers.

VARIATION: MONOCHROME

Color variation
A color palette of black, white, and shades of gray makes an interesting contrast to the brightly colored palette.

4 Second butterfly: the second butterfly uses heart motifs. Again, complete the body first. Then place the center of the hearts.

5 Work outward for each heart, banding around the center in each color.

6 Now outline the wings with a double line of very small, square-cut tiles and finish with a checkerboard fill, fitting each piece to check its accuracy before gluing it down.

7 Third butterfly: once again complete the body of the butterfly first.

8 Now place the centers of the circles.

9 Surround these with radial fills of carefully dovetailed tiles.

10 Finally, complete the wings with a crackle fill.

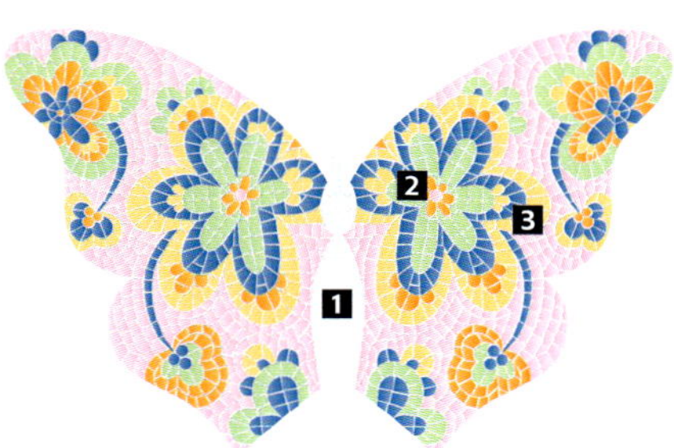

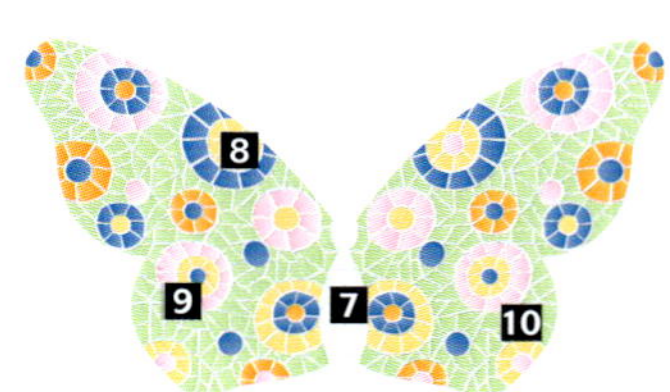

ORDER OF WORK **KEY**

TILE CUTTING AND PLACEMENT GUIDE

COLOR PALETTE

Main panel Variation

Suggested dimensions

To scale and transfer the design follow the techniques described on pages 18–19. Size of each butterfly: 13⅜ x 20 in. (34 x 51 cm).

PANEL TRANSFER GRID

PANEL TRANSFER GRID

COLOR PALETTE

Main panel **Variation**

Color variation

This version of the design is warmer and more reminiscent of fall as the leaves of the vine start to go brown.

VARIATION: FALL COLORS

MOSAIC 12: GRAPEVINE

THIS IS A LATE SUMMER VINE BEFORE THE LEAVES TURN BROWN, BUT IN A COOL COLOR PALETTE WITH WHITE GRAPES AND SUBTLE BLUES AND GREENS. IF YOU WANT TO WORK THIS DESIGN AS A REPEATING BORDER ALONG A WALL, THEN YOU WILL NEED TO EXTEND THE DRAWING SO THAT THE MAIN BRANCH OF THE VINE MEETS IN THE CORRECT PLACE AT THE START OF THE NEXT REPEAT.

Skill level: **2**

Materials

Standard-size vitreous tiles
Estimating tile quantities, **see page 11**

Order of work

1 Start with the bunches of grapes, placing a highlight tile of white, or a light pearlescent hue; then, if you have two tones of the grape color that are very close, surround the highlight with the lighter tone.

2 Lay the veins of the leaves first, giving them a fine, pointy shape. The fill works around the beautiful symmetrical shape of the leaf: study a real vine leaf if you can.

3 The main stem requires neat, precise cutting to make a smooth curve.

4 For the curly fronds cut the tile pieces as narrow as you can.

5 Use a regular, rectangular fill for the background.

FOLD OUT THE FLAP

TILE CUTTING AND PLACEMENT GUIDE

Suggested dimensions

To scale and transfer the design follow the techniques described on pages 18–19. Size of design: 8⅝ x 20⅝ in. (22 x 52.5 cm).

MOSAIC 13: CACTI

SUITABLE FOR A SUNROOM OR GARDEN AREA, THIS DESIGN WILL WORK WELL BEHIND ALL SORTS OF PLANTS AND VEGETATION. THE HOT, PINK COLOR PALETTE GIVES A SULTRY, LUSCIOUS FEEL. USE BRIGHTLY-COLORED CERAMIC TILES, PERHAPS COMBINED WITH BROKEN PIECES OF TERRACOTTA POTS, WHICH YOU COULD ADORN WITH HAND-PAINTED MOTIFS ONCE THE PIECE HAS BEEN GROUTED.

Skill level: **2**

Materials

Standard-size vitreous tiles or household ceramic tiles

Estimating tile quantities, **see page 11**

VARIATION: TEMPERATE PALETTE

ORDER OF WORK **KEY**

Order of work

1 Begin with the patterns on the shelf, then the main shelf fill which follows the curves of the plant fronds.

2 Move on to the zigzag pattern on the first pot, then complete the horizontal stripes before tiling the bulk of the pot.

3 For the cactus spikes, use sharp, triangular cuts, then surround these with a crackle fill of green tiles.

4 The second pot is more complex: place the circular-cut tiles first then lay bands of tapered tiles around these so that they dovetail neatly together. Finish with a background crackle fill that contrasts nicely with the pots on either side.

5 The short, squat cactus combines sharp triangular and rectangular tiles for the lower half, with softer, petal-shaped cuts for the crowning flower.

6 The way you tile the third pot should echo the first, both in the colors and the size and cuts of the tile pieces. Again start with the patterned areas first.

7 Complete each dagger-like leaf of the third cactus one at a time, starting with the foremost one and working backward. Jse two tones of green that are similar in hue.

8 Finally, do a simple grid fill in a vibrant color for the background. Cut the tiles so they fit neatly round the pots and plarts leaving ar even space for grout.

Color variation

This variation is slightly cooler and less tropical with the colors of the pots toned down. Yellow is a good alternative if you find the pink too garish.

PANEL TRANSFER GRID

Suggested dimensions

To scale and transfer the design follow the techniques described on pages 18–19. Size of design: 19⅛ x 28½ in. (48.5 x 72 cm).

COLOR PALETTE

TILE CUTTING AND PLACEMENT GUIDE

MOSAIC 14: FANTASY FLOWERS

THE FLORAL MOTIF AND THE HOT TROPICAL COLORS IN THIS PIECE MAKE IT IDEALLY SUITED FOR A SUNROOM OR GARDEN ROOM.

VARIATION: RICH AND STRIKING

Skill level: **4**

Materials

Standard-size vitreous tiles
Estimating tile quantities, **see page 11**

Order of work

1 Create the individual flower heads, working on the inner, circular centers first.

2 Complete the stalks and curly fronds.

3 Cut and place the leaves.

4 Complete the butterflies. You can substitute millefiori tiles for the small circular tiles that are used for the wing details.

5 The flying bird is a key element of the composition. The white dove could be replaced with an exotically colored parakeet.

6 Create the perching bird at the foot of the design.

7 Place all the berries using small, circular-cut tiles.

8 Take particular care to make the arcs that create the point of the frame equal and balanced.

9 Complete the background fill: here a checkerboard is suggested but you could use an irregular or crackle fill if you want a different effect.

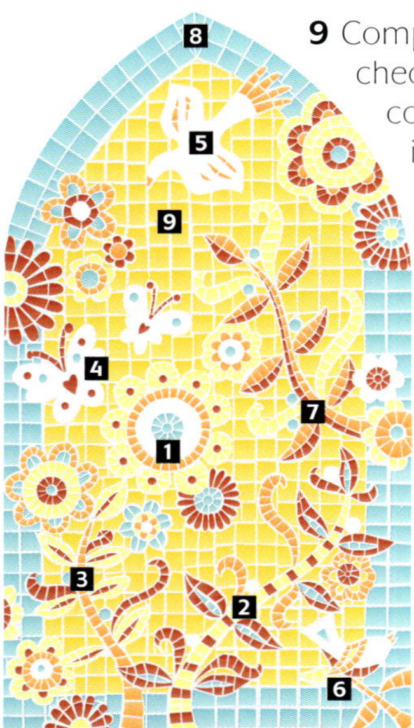

ORDER OF WORK **KEY**

PANEL TRANSFER GRID

Color variation

Try using a richer color palette of warm browns, terracottas, reds, and purples.

COLOR PALETTE

Main panel	Variation

Suggested dimensions

To scale and transfer the design follow the techniques described on pages 18–19. Size of design: 26¾ x 14¼ in. (68 x 36 cm).

TILE CUTTING AND PLACEMENT GUIDE

MOSAIC 15: PEACOCK

THE DRAMATIC SHAPE OF THIS PEACOCK PRODUCES A DESIGN THAT IS TALL AND THIN, AND WHICH GIVES THE BIRD A HAUGHTY AIR. ALTHOUGH QUITE NATURALISTIC, THE EFFECT IS ALMOST ABSTRACT BECAUSE OF THE RICHNESS OF THE PEACOCK'S PLUMAGE. YOU CAN ADD TO THE OPULENCE OF THE PIECE BY USING GOLD TILES IN THE BIRD'S TAIL, OR WHEN THE TILES HAVE BEEN GROUTED, BY STICKING JEWELS OR OTHER MATERIALS ONTO THE SURFACE OF THESE AREAS OF PLUMAGE.

Skill level: **2**

Materials

Standard-size vitreous tiles (preferably some metallic or with gold streaks), jewels, diamantés
Estimating tile quantities, **see page 11**

PANEL TRANSFER GRID

Suggested dimensions
To scale and transfer the design follow the techniques described on pages 18–19. Size of design: 27½ x 10¼ in. (70 x 26 cm).

Order of work

1 Draw up the outlines of the design strongly, then tile the heart-shaped motif at the center of each of the tail feathers.

2 Next, tile the circular surround to these heart shapes, then each further band of color to complete each tail feather. If you have some metallic or metal-streaked tiles, use these to give the final band particular emphasis.

3 The eye has a dark pupil surrounded by an almond shape of either white or light-toned tiles. Cut and place the few tiles that make up the eye very carefully as this is a central point of focus for the whole picture.

4 Tile the crown of the head, then work downward completing the plumage on the bird's back—this is made up of parallel, tapering bands of tiles, with the vertical and horizontal edges aligned to give a smooth, even fill.

5 The breast of the bird is filled with a contrasting crackle fill—although the tones and colors used should be as close together as possible to achieve a unifying effect.

6 The bird's crest consists of "stalks" of thinly cut shards of tiles, each topped with a spear-like shape cut from an individual tile. Again, this detail is a strong feature of the design so draw the shape carefully with a washable felt-tip pen, then cut out each one as accurately as possible.

7 Each flower radiates from a circular-cut tile, surrounded by petals of more circles, each cut from just one tile.

8 The background fill uses the darkest possible, ebony black tiles, which seem to follow and cloak the shape of the bird.

VARIATION: NEGATIVE

Color variation

This version is like a negative of the first, with an almost ghost-like quality, achieved by using tiles with fine pearlescent shades.

ORDER OF WORK **KEY**

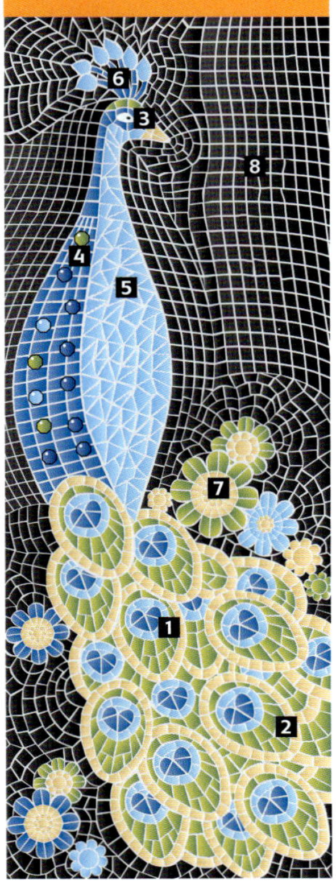

COLOR PALETTE

Main panel **Variation**

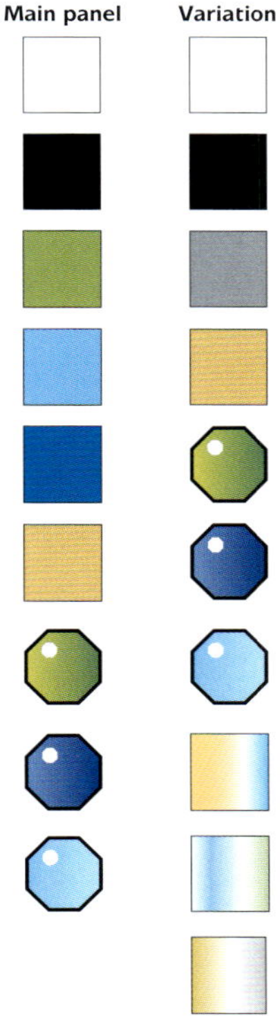

TILE CUTTING AND PLACEMENT GUIDE

MOSAIC 16: ROOSTER

THIS DESIGN TAKES ITS INSPIRATION FROM THE HOT COLOR PALETTE AND DESIGN MOTIFS OF FRENCH PROVENÇAL POTTERY AND TEXTILES. IT HAS A SUNNY, BRIGHT FEEL THAT WORKS WELL IN A TRADITIONAL KITCHEN WITH OTHER "WARM" MATERIALS SUCH AS WOOD AND TERRACOTTA TILES.

Skill level: **3**

Materials

Standard-size vitreous tiles
Estimating tile quantities, **see page 11**

Order of work

1 Start with the rooster's beady eye, followed by the beak and comb.

2 Work your way down the plumage, creating the puffy chest. If using ceramic tiles, try cutting large, tapered pieces to create the effect of individual feathers.

3 To add contrast, detail the small feathers on the bird's back with small, carefully cut pieces of more intensely colored tiles.

4 As you build the tail, work in concentric circles to accentuate the plumpness of the bird.

5 Take care to get the feet right: it may take several attempts to cut and position the tile pieces before the shape looks natural.

6 Complete the flamboyant tail plumage.

7 The bees are optional; either complete them now before going on to the background, or leave them out.

8 The lavender around the bird's feet "grounds" the composition, and adds to the Provençal feel.

9 The clouds break up the background and add tonal contrast.

10 Start the sun from the edge of the cloud using a fill of concentric rings completed by triangular shapes.

11 The background is a simple checkerboard to provide unity to the different elements of the picture.

12 The border is based on an olive motif: start by cutting the circles and place them equidistantly, before adding the leaves and the fill in between. If cutting in glass, try and keep the uncut edge of the tiles facing outward from the border to make the finished piece easier to handle.

VARIATION: COOL AND SOPHISTICATED

Color variation

This blue palette retains a "French" atmosphere, but with a cooler, perhaps more sophisticated feel. This variation would work effectively set in deep yellow or ochre tiles, to bring out the contrasting blues.

ORDER OF WORK **KEY**

TILE CUTTING AND PLACEMENT GUIDE

PANEL TRANSFER GRID

Suggested dimensions

To scale and transfer the design follow the techniques described on pages 18–19. Size of design: 17 x 19¼ in. (43 x 49 cm).

COLOR PALETTE

Main panel | Variation

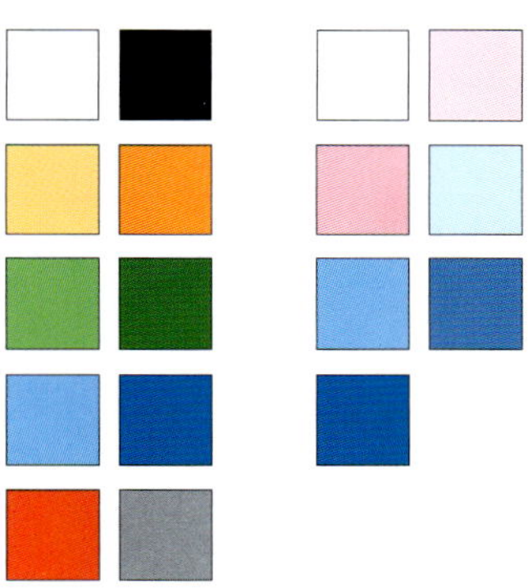

MOSAIC 17: DELFT TILES

THIS PIECE IMITATES THE CLASSIC, BLUE AND WHITE HAND-PAINTED TILES THAT ORIGINATED FROM DELFT IN HOLLAND FROM THE 16TH CENTURY. THE DESIGN USES MOSAIC TILES TO RECREATE EACH INDIVIDUAL DELFT TILE. YOU CAN REARRANGE THE TILES VERTICALLY OR HORIZONTALLY TO MAKE A DIFFERENT PANEL OR RESEARCH ALTERNATIVE PATTERNS FROM THE MANY BOOKS ON DELFT TILES.

Skill level: **3**

Materials

Standard-size vitreous tiles
Estimating tile quantities, **see page 11**

1 Work from left to right, taking care to center each design by drawing diagonals between opposite corners. Begin with the circular center to the first tile.

2, 10, & 12 Again, draw guidelines to help achieve the symmetry of the design. Make fine cuts to create the complex, curved outlines of the shapes. Keep checking to see that you are keeping each axis of the design balanced—lift and replace any tile that looks lopsided.

3 You can do all the corner motifs at once, placing them carefully on the guide lines.

ORDER OF WORK **KEY**

4, 5, 7, 9, & 11 All require the same care with marking up the center point of the design and building the design out along two axes which are at right angles.

6–8 Draw a double line for these outlines and carefully fit the tiles to this width, nibbling off small chunks with tile nippers as necessary. "Dovetail" the ends of the tiles so that the grouting gap between the tiles is even despite the curved path the tiles are following.

13 Finally, complete the background of each tile, moving from left to right. Lay the edge of each tile first so that the grid of squares is really emphasized, then fill inward to the central motif.

VARIATION: REVERSED

Color variation

The second color sequence reverses the dark blue and white palette. You could also use terracotta colors as these were also popular with the Delft tile-makers.

PANEL TRANSFER GRID

Suggested dimensions

To scale and transfer the design follow the techniques described on pages 18–19. Size of design: 12½ x 17¼ in. (32 x 44 cm).

COLOR PALETTE

Main panel | Variation

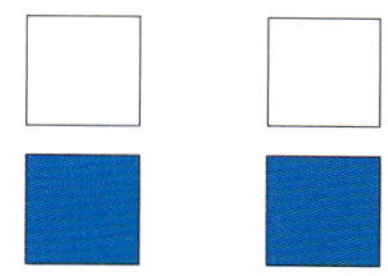

TILE CUTTING AND PLACEMENT GUIDE

MOSAIC 18: SPIRALING FLOWERS

THE CERAMIC TILES USED IN THIS DESIGN ALLOW YOU TO CREATE LARGE, STRONG AREAS OF BRIGHT COLOR. MAKE EACH SECTION OF THE DESIGN THE SIZE OF A STANDARD WALL TILE, SO YOU CAN INTEGRATE EACH ONE WITHIN A LARGE TILED AREA, SUCH AS A BATHROOM OR KITCHEN WALL.

TRY USING PATTERNED OR TEXTURED TILES. THIS VERSION USES FIVE "COOL" COLORS: TONES OF BLUE, A PALE GREEN, AND WHITE.

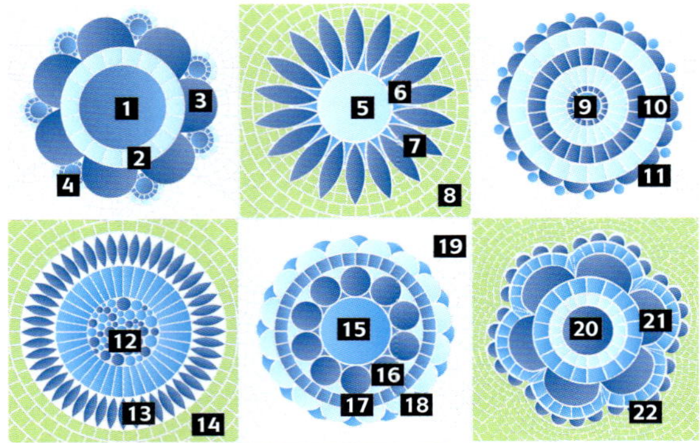

ORDER OF WORK **KEY**

Skill level: **4**

Materials

Household ceramic tiles
Estimating tile quantities, **see page 11**

Suggested dimensions

To scale and transfer the design follow the techniques described on pages 18–19.
Size of design: 20⅝ x 30 in. (52.5 x 76 cm).

PANEL TRANSFER GRID

Order of work

1 Start with the top left flower: cut a large circle from a single tile; mark it first using a washable felt-tip pen, drawing around a circular object, such as a cup or glass. Mark and then cut a square as close to the edge of the circle as possible, then nibble round the outline. Smooth off any irregular edges using coarse sandpaper.

2 Complete the next band, dovetailing carefully tapered oblong shapes together.

3 The petals are made using a suitably sized circular object as a template; then nibble a convex curve to fit around the center of the flower.

4 More small circles are placed between these petals, then these are completed with a fill, and a fan-type background that follows the shape of the flower.

5 The second flower: again start with a large circle at the center, then place the large petals. These are made from narrow rectangles of tile; with a washable felt-tip pen draw a center line lengthways as a guide, then draw the outline of the petal, making both sides as symmetrical as possible.

6 At the base of the petals, place a small triangular "filler."

7 Start with larger triangles to fill the wider space between the other end of the petals. You will need to shape these to fit the curves and the outside outline.

8 The background consists of bands of tiles following the circle of the outline.

9 The third flower: create this with a small circular tile center, then successive bands of tiles tapered so their edges neatly butt together.

10 A final band of semicircular tiles and polka-dots adds interest.

11 Finish with an outer fill in a scalloped pattern that follows the wavy outline of the flower.

12 The fourth flower: first

TILE CUTTING AND PLACEMENT GUIDE

draw a large circle, then cut lots of little circles of different size, playing around with them to fit tightly together within your drawn outline.

13 Surround the center with a band of long tapered oblongs, then a band of small petals (smaller versions of those used in the second flower).

14 Finish with a simple radial fill.

15 The fifth flower: place another large circular center, then surround this with a ring of smaller circles.

16 In the gaps, cut small triangular fillers, curving the edges for a neater fit.

17 Now lay a band of simple, square-cut tiles to establish a strong circular outline.

18 Against this outline, place a band of semicircular petals with more triangular "gap fillers."

19 Use another scalloped fill for the background.

20 The sixth flower: a simple circle and two radial bands create a strong center.

21 Surround the center with six semicircular petals.

22 The remaining details must be laid in a wavy form around this central flower shape—a band of square-cut tiles, then small semicircles, finally a surrounding fan-like fill of more square-cut tiles.

COLOR PALETTE

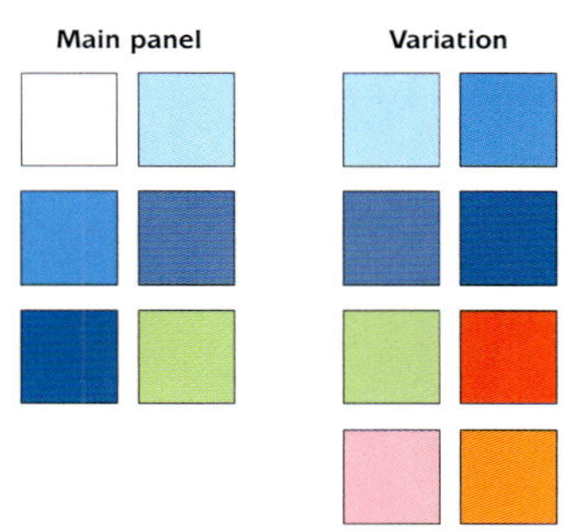

Color variation
Larger, hotter color palette with hot pinks, mauves, and red.

VARIATION: HOT COLORS

MOSAIC 19: PLATE RACK

A RELATIVELY SIMPLE DESIGN THAT UTILIZES "TROMPE L'OEIL" EFFECTS OF SHADOW TO CREATE A THREE-DIMENSIONAL IMPRESSION. WHOLE PLATES ARE INCORPORATED INTO THE FINISHED PIECE SO IT IS VITAL TO USE A SPECIAL CERAMIC ADHESIVE CAPABLE OF SUPPORTING THEIR WEIGHT. IN THE FIRST EXAMPLE THE COLOR BLUE PREDOMINATES. YOU COULD ALSO INTEGRATE OTHER "FOUND OBJECTS," SUCH AS SMALL ORNAMENTS, INTO THE DESIGN.

Skill level: **2**

Materials

Standard-size vitreous tiles and "found objects" (plates)
Estimating tile quantities, **see page 11**

PANEL TRANSFER GRID

VARIATION: EARTHY

Color variation

As an alternative try a more "earthy" palette that will blend in well in a kitchen with pine furniture.

Suggested dimensions

To scale and transfer the design follow the techniques described on pages 18–19. Size of design: 35 x 26½ in. (89 x 67.5 cm).

ORDER OF WORK **KEY**

COLOR PALETTE

Main panel **Variation**

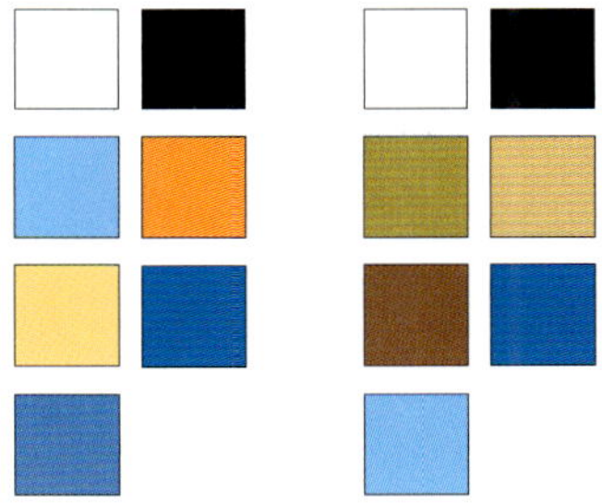

Order of work

1 Cut the shape of the plate rack in MDF and then tile the frame and decorative molding along the top before completing the rest of the horizontal shelves.

2 Fill the shadow areas using darker-toned tiles.

3 Move on to the cat: follow the usual order for animals/figures, completing the smaller details such as the eyes and nose, then the stripes and tail, before filling in the larger, surrounding areas.

4 Complete the background; then grout, clean, and allow everything to dry thoroughly.

5 Before gluing on the plates check that all surfaces are clean and grease-free to ensure the glue works. It is vital to do this while the piece is horizontal. Leave plenty of time for the glue to set before hanging the piece on the wall.

TILE CUTTING AND PLACEMENT GUIDE

MOSAIC 20: CAKE STANDS

CAKE STANDS HAVE MADE A COMEBACK AND THIS PIECE, WITH ITS GARISH PINKS AND EXAGGERATED HIGHLIGHTS ON THE JELLO AND CHERRIES, RECREATES THE KITSCH OF A 1950s AMERICAN DINER. YOU COULD ENHANCE THE "TROMPE L'OEIL" EFFECT, AS IF THE STANDS ARE ON A REAL SHELF, BY DARKENING THE SHADOW UNDER THE SHELF.

Skill level: **2**

Materials

Standard-size vitreous tiles
Estimating tile quantities, **see page 11**

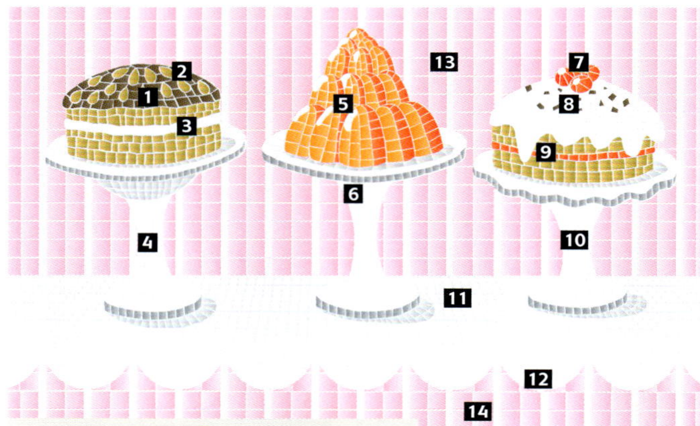

ORDER OF WORK **KEY**

Order of work

1 Start with the left-hand cake, cutting out and placing the shapes of the almonds.

2 Move on to the surrounding chocolate frosting.

3 Cut the edges of the cream filling so that it looks uneven like cream oozing out, rather than a straight ribbon surrounding the cake.

4 Cut and lay the tiles for the first cake stand.

5 Moving on to the jello, place the highlights first, creating smooth, rounded shapes. Then use colors of two similar tones to create the mass of the jello. Again nibble away at the edge of each tile to get a rounded effect.

6 Now complete the second cake stand.

7 For the last cake, begin with the cherries and again accentuate the highlights.

8 Place the sprinkles on the top of the cake then tile round these to create the icing.

9 Finish as for the first cake, creating a soft, oozing, central jam layer.

VARIATION: 1960s RETRO

COLOR PALETTE

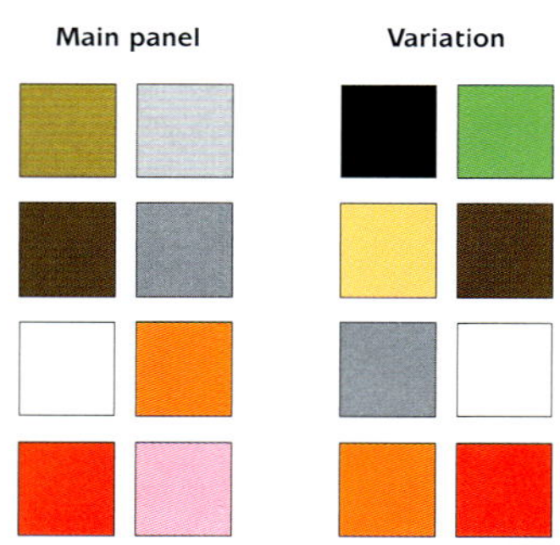

Color variation

Still a "retro" look but now more 1960s, with the strong black and white background.

10 Do the last cake stand.

11 Tile the shelf on which the cakes are standing, carefully following the perspective lines that help give a 3-D effect.

12 Cut the decorative frill at the front of the shelf, following the curves as shown in the drawing.

13–14 Finish off the background, completing all the thin stripes first, then filling the areas in between. To make things easier space the stripes to exact multiples of tile-with-grout widths to minimize the amount of cutting required.

PANEL TRANSFER GRID

Suggested dimensions

To scale and transfer the design follow the techniques described on pages 18–19.
Size of design: 20⅝ x 32¾ in. (52.5 x 83 cm).

TILE CUTTING AND PLACEMENT GUIDE

MOSAIC 21: VEGETABLES

A STYLIZED RENDITION OF VEGETABLES, THIS DESIGN REINTERPRETS THE STRONG FORMS OF COMMON VEGETABLES INTO MORE ABSTRACTED SHAPES, AND USES STRONG COLORS TO MAKE THEM MORE TWO-DIMENSIONAL. THE PIECE COULD ALSO BE DONE AS A FRIEZE, WITH THE VEGETABLES LAID OUT IN A SINGLE ROW ALONG A WALL, OR ISOLATED BY RECTANGULAR BACKGROUNDS OF DIFFERENT COLORS. THIS VERSION USES FIVE COLORS, STRONGLY GROUPED AROUND COOLER BLUES.

Skill level: **1**

Materials

Standard-size vitreous tiles
Estimating tile quantities, **see page 11**

ORDER OF WORK **KEY**

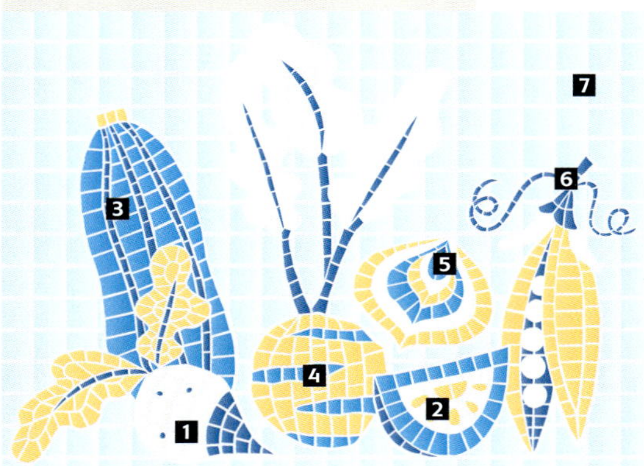

Order of work

1 Start with the radish, placing the small markings first, then work outward filling the body, and then tapering down to the pointed tip. Keep the leaves curvy using nibbling cuts to give a smooth outline.

2 Begin the tomato with the seeds: each one is cut from a single tile, then work outward, finishing with a band of tiles that effectively outlines the shape.

3 The squash is laid in vertical bands; do the narrower stripes first, then fill between with tile pieces almost a single width across.

4 Begin the kohlrabi with the markings and then fill the body. The leaves have a central vein; cut the tiles for this as thinly as possible, then use curvy cuts for the remainder of each leaf.

5 The onion is filled from the top center, working out in rings and cutting with precision to keep the neat shape.

6 The oversized peapod begins with the cap and delicate tendrils that need the finest possible cuts to create tiny shards of t le. Do the foremost half of the pod first, then the peas that are slightly hidden, then, finally, the "background" half of the pod.

7 Complete the piece with a surrounding checkerboard fill.

COLOR PALETTE

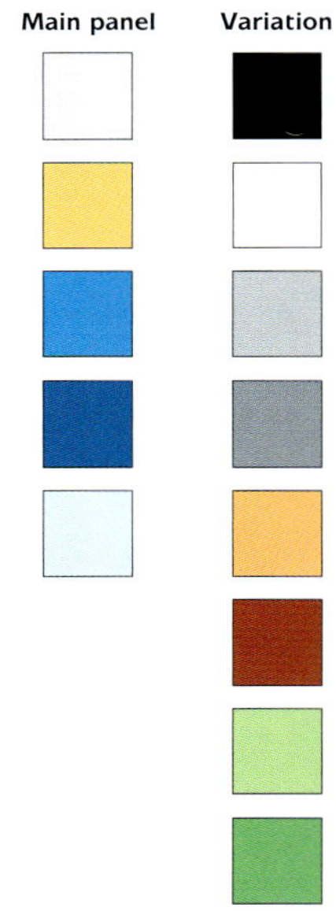

PANEL TRANSFER GRID

TILE CUTTING AND PLACEMENT GUIDE

VARIATION: NATURALISTIC

Color variation

This alternative color palette uses a more naturalistic set of colors, with warmer greens and earth tones, but still in a highly stylized way.

Suggested dimensions

To scale and transfer the design follow the techniques described on pages 18–19.
Size of design: 13⅜ x 17¾ in. (34 x 45 cm).

MOSAIC 22: PENGUINS

THIS IS A GOOD MOSAIC FOR A BEGINNER TO TACKLE. A SIMPLE COLOR PALETTE MEANS YOU CAN FOCUS ON YOUR CUTTING TECHNIQUE AND FITTING TILES TO THE STRONG OUTLINE. THIS DESIGN WORKS JUST AS WELL AT ALMOST ANY SIZE.

Skill level: **1**

Materials

Standard-size vitreous tiles
Estimating title quantities, **see page 11**

ORDER OF WORK **KEY**

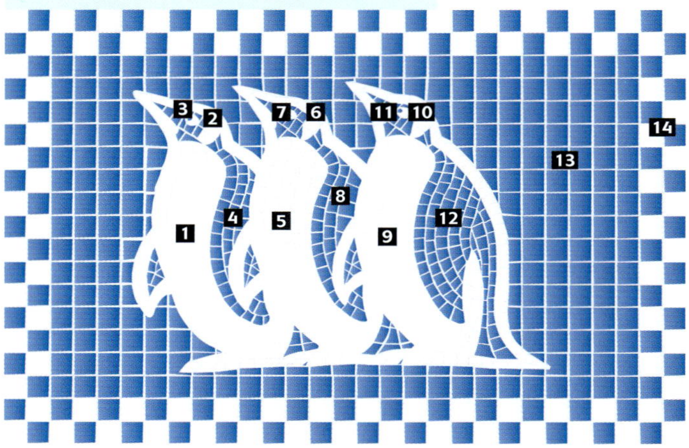

PANEL TRANSFER GRID

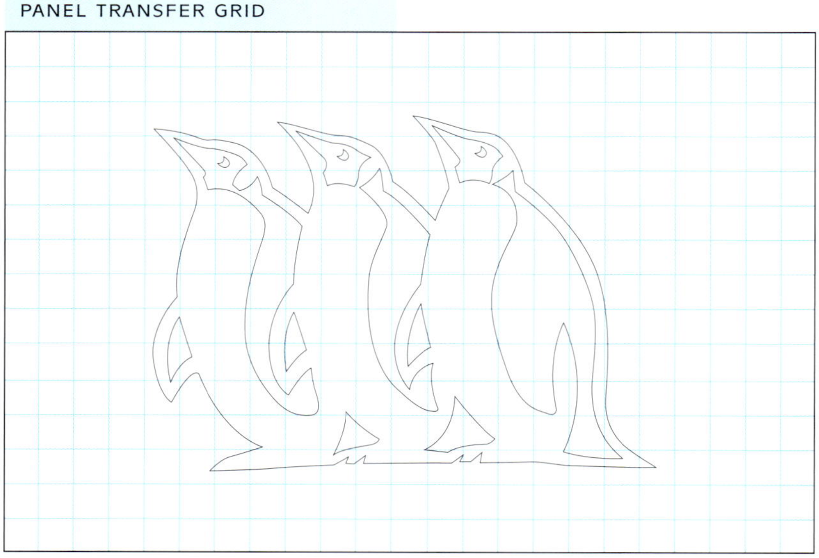

Order of work

1 Start by filling the white area of the first penguin's stomach, laying the tiles to follow and accentuate the curved shape.

2 Continue the white tiles around the outline of the head.

3 Place the white tile of the eye: to create this shape, cut a circle, then use your nippers to make a notch. Alternatively, cut two separate pieces to make the shape of the eye.

4 Take your blue tiles and fill in the head and wings.

5–12 Repeat for the other two penguins, following the same order as above.

13 Fill in the background. A solid, square fill provides a contrast to the curved shape of the penguins.

14 Finally, frame the piece with a checkerboard pattern of whole tiles, alternating the two colors of the design.

Suggested dimensions

To scale and transfer the design follow the techniques described on pages 18–19. Size of design: 15 x 22⅝ in. (38 x 57.5 cm).

TILE CUTTING AND PLACEMENT GUIDE

VARIATION: REVERSED

COLOR PALETTE

Main panel | Variation

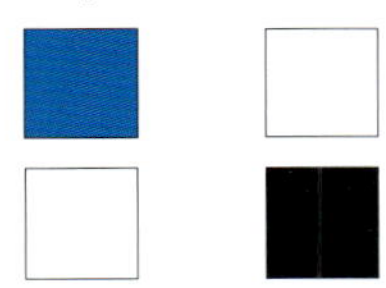

Color variation

Here the design has been "reversed"—it works just as beautifully when rendered as a negative. Take care to achieve the outline of the wings with more delicately cut tiles.

MOSAIC 23: BOATS AT SEA

THIS SOOTHING, FLOWING DESIGN WORKS WELL IN A BATHROOM. HERE, SMALL FISH HAVE BEEN INCLUDED BUT THESE COULD BE OMITTED IF YOU WANT A MORE "CLASSICAL" DESIGN.

Skill level: **3**

Materials

Standard-size vitreous tiles
Estimating tile quantities, **see page 11**

TILE CUTTING AND PLACEMENT GUIDE

Order of work

1 Start with the sails: concentrate on the curved fills and patterns just as much as the outline to give a full, billowing effect.

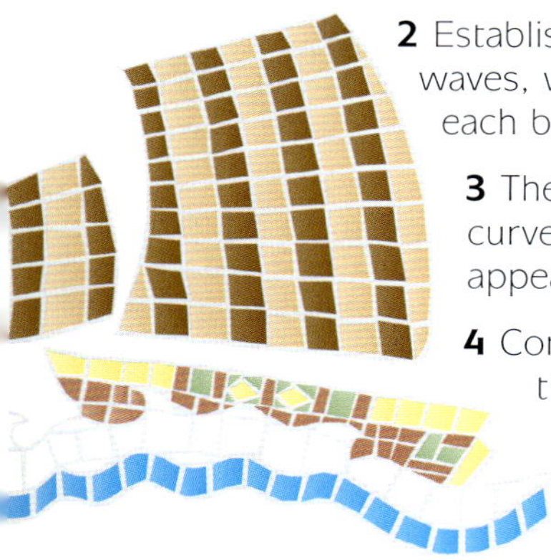

2 Establish the breaking (white) waves, which form the base for each boat.

3 The hulls need to be subtly curved and cut so that they appear to sit on the waves.

4 Complete each cloud from the center outward, working in concentric circles.

5 If you want to include fish in your mosaic, cut and position them now.

6 Fill in the sea: start from the horizon and work downward, completing a band of each color at a time.

7 Cut and place the tile pieces for the birds using thin shards of tile.

8 Finally, fill in the sky, continuing the concentric patterns established by the clouds.

ORDER OF WORK **KEY**

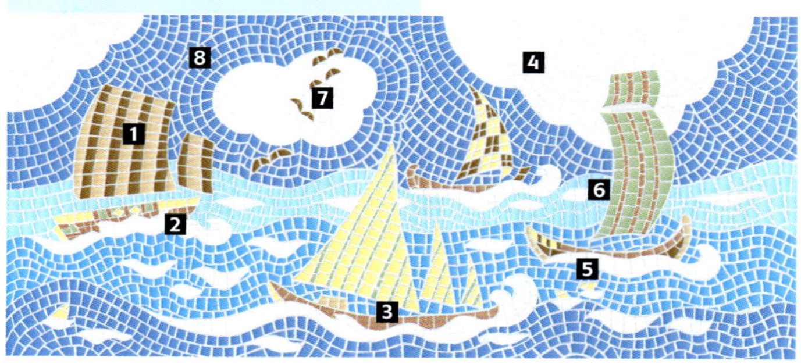

Suggested dimensions

To scale and transfer the design follow the techniques described on pages 18–19. Size of design: 16½ x 37½ in. (42 x 95 cm).

COLOR PALETTE

Color variation
The second version has a more "Mediterranean" palette with green-turquoise sea and sky and terracotta and pink sails.

VARIATION: MEDITERRANEAN

PANEL TRANSFER GRID

MOSAIC 24: MERMAID & DOLPHIN

THIS DESIGN IS IDEAL FOR THE WALLS OF A SHOWER OR BATHROOM PROVIDED YOU USE WATERPROOF GROUT. SKILL IS REQUIRED TO CUT THE FLOWING LINES OF THE MERMAID'S LONG, SEAWEED-LIKE HAIR. ACCURATE CUTTING AND PLACEMENT OF TILES IS ALSO NEEDED TO ACHIEVE THE FINE DETAIL OF THE FISH DANCING IN AND OUT OF HER TRESSES, AND THE MERMAID'S SMALL, ALMOST HIDDEN FACE. AS A FINISHING TOUCH YOU CAN ADD GLASS BEADS TO APPEAR LIKE WATER DROPLETS AFTER GROUTING.

Skill level: **3**

Materials

Standard-size vitreous tiles
Estimating tile quantities, **see page 11**

Color variation

The second version has a bit more impact with a stronger use of color—you could use the fish to pick up an accent color from the surrounding room.

VARIATION: BRIGHT AND VIBRANT

Order of work

1 As with all designs involving figures it is vital to get the face absolutely right, so tackle this first. Faces in profile are a little easier; however, be prepared to reject plenty of tiles before you are happy that the eyes and nose are right-on.

ORDER OF WORK **KEY**

2–3 Move on to the fish in the mermaid's hair. Depending on the scale at which you are working, you can put in the detail of individual scales on each fish. Once they are completed tackle the hair in segments, cutting and placing the tiles to suggest the flow of the hair, rather than treating it as a flat area.

4 Next do the arms; the hands are a tricky detail to render well, like the face, so be patient, and reject any tiles that miss the necessary delicacy.

5 Place the dolphin's eye before filling the darker, upper area of its body, then move on to the softer color of the underside.

6 The scales on the mermaid's tail need to appear to overlap, so begin from the top and work down. The component tiles of each scale need careful "nibbling" to ensure a smooth, rounded edge.

7 The tail is difficult. There are lots of tapering areas next to each other; to get a smooth, flowing result requires very accurate drawing and cutting.

8 The background is broken up by strong, horizontal waves; complete these first, cutting your tiles to work with the curve, rather than against it.

TILE CUTTING AND PLACEMENT GUIDE

9 The little semi-circular shapes—they could be shells, bubbles, or seaweed—add interest but are optional, so leave them out if you want the picture to be less busy.

10 Finally, the background of the sea: although plain, the fill should undulate in harmony with the waves. Once grouted you could add glass beads to the surface of the mosaic, fixing them onto the tiles with a waterproof glue.

COLOR PALETTE

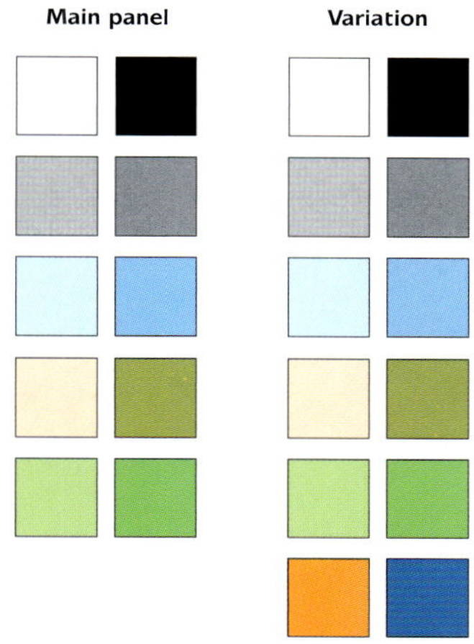

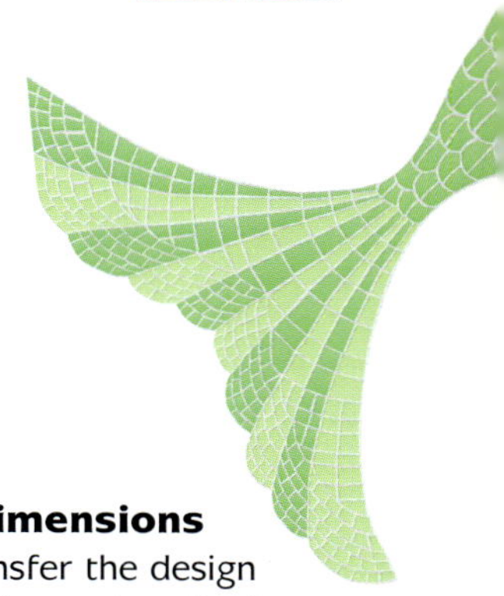

Suggested dimensions

To scale and transfer the design follow the techniques described on pages 18–19. Size of design: 31 x 20 in. (79 x 51 cm).

PANEL TRANSFER GRID

MOSAIC 25: BATH-TIME NUMBERS

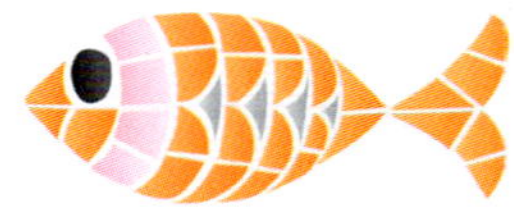

THIS IS A FAIRLY EASY SEQUENCE OF SIMPLE, BOLD DESIGNS. EACH NUMERAL AND ITS ILLUSTRATION IS SET IN A PYRAMID SHAPE, SUGGESTING CHILDREN'S BUILDING BLOCKS. ALTERNATIVELY, YOU COULD DO A SIMPLE LINEAR SEQUENCE, EXTENDING IT WITH MORE NUMBERS AND OTHER REPEAT MOTIFS. AS THIS MOSAIC IS IDEAL FOR YOUNG CHILDREN, YOU MAY NOT WANT TO MAKE IT PERMANENT BY APPLYING DIRECTLY TO A WALL. INSTEAD, COMPLETE EACH SECTION ON A PIECE OF MDF AND HANG THESE LIKE A PICTURE WITH A WIRE OR HOOK SCREWED TO THE BACK.

Skill level: **2**

Materials

Standard-size vitreous tiles or household ceramic tiles
Estimating tile quantities, **see page 11**

Order of work

1 Start with the duck, placing the eye first.

2 Next, do the rabbit in front of the number 2, again starting with the eye, and then the inside of the ear.

3 Complete the second rabbit on the foot of the 2.

4 When creating the fish, start from the mouth and work backward toward the tail.

5–7 Block in the numbers: this is the strength of the design, so concentrate on even outlines and strong, even fills.

8 Tuck in the third fish behind the number.

9 Go back to the bathwater for the duck. Do the bubbles, cut from circles, then fill the area beneath them.

10 Complete the first number with a traditional checkerboard background.

11–12 The hills in the rabbit picture need a flowing fill that follows the curve of their outline. Use alternating stripes for a "ploughed field" effect.

13 A flat fill for the sky completes the number 2.

14 Finish the sea around the number 3 using alternate ribbons of color.

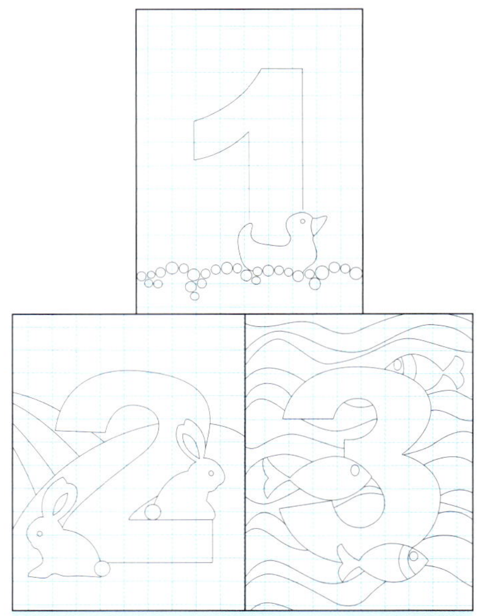

PANEL TRANSFER GRID

Suggested dimensions

To scale and transfer the design follow the techniques described on pages 18–19. Size of design: 25¼ x 18½ in. (64 x 47 cm).

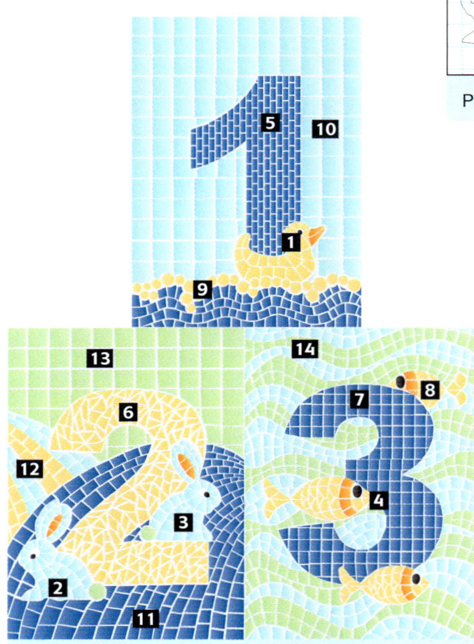

ORDER OF WORK **KEY**

COLOR PALETTE

Main panel **Variation**

TILE CUTTING AND PLACEMENT GUIDE

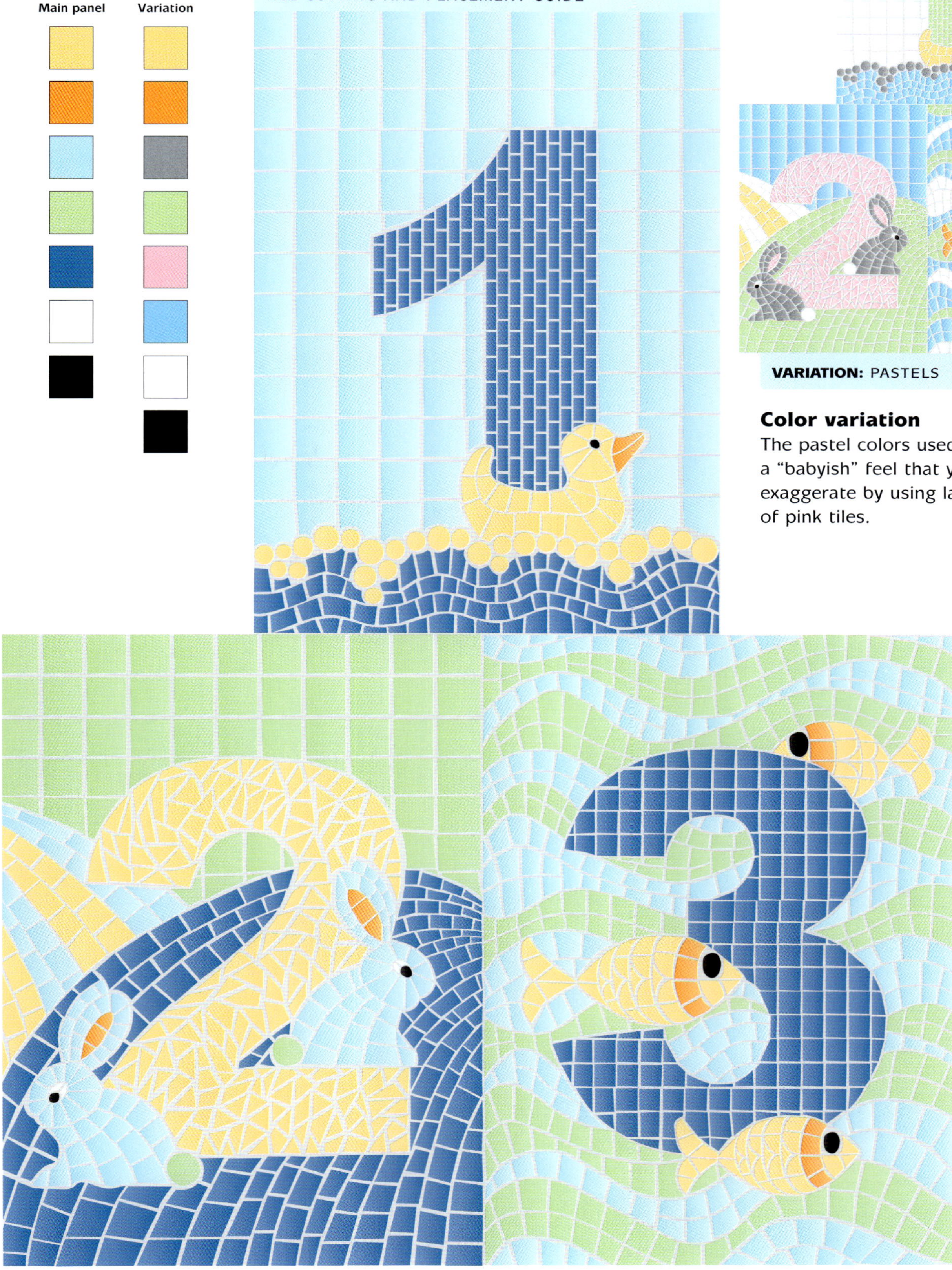

VARIATION: PASTELS

Color variation

The pastel colors used here have a "babyish" feel that you can exaggerate by using larger quantities of pink tiles.

MOSAIC 26: TERNS

THIS NATURALISTIC AND CHALLENGING PIECE REQUIRES DELICATE SHADES TO CREATE LIGHT AND SHADOW. SELECT TILES CAREFULLY TO COMPOSE THE SUBTLE GRADATION OF THE SKY. THE SENSE OF DISTANCE IS CREATED BY LIGHTENING THE TONES OF OBJECTS THE FURTHER AWAY THEY ARE. AVOID USING BLACK TILES FOR THE SHADOWS; INSTEAD USE VERY DARK TONES OF COLORS, SUCH AS GREENS, BLUES, AND BROWNS.

ORDER OF WORK **KEY**

Skill level: **3**

Materials

Standard-size vitreous tiles
Estimating tile quantities, **see page 11**

PANEL TRANSFER GRID

Order of work

1 Complete the terns in order, beginning with the nearest first. Start with the eyes, beak, and crest, then flow the plumage down from the head.

2 Use a scalloped effect for the feathers of the wings.

3 Use very precise cuts and careful positioning to achieve the delicately forked tail feathers.

4 If following a naturalistic color palette, select subtly darker tones to create the shadowing effect on the sand beneath the tern. Reject any tiles that are too dark and contrasting.

5–6 The breakwater posts can be kept simple, or embellished to suggest barnacles and seaweed. Keep the shadowing delicate and not too dark.

7 Place the foreground pebbles and shells. If working in glass tiles, use some pearlescent finishes.

8 The sand is a simple, flat fill, but be selective with the tiles to get the sense of depth and recession.

9–10 Finish off with the circling birds, then complete the sky, carefully choosing and arranging tiles that create the right gradation.

Suggested dimensions

To scale and transfer the design follow the techniques described on pages 18–19. Size of design: 25 x 21½ in. (63.5 x 54.5 cm).

Color variation

This color palette simplifies the piece by replacing the subtle shades with areas of flat, strong color. The end result has a different impact, but is easier to undertake and requires a smaller palette of tiles.

VARIATION: SIMPLIFIED SHADING

TILE CUTTING AND PLACEMENT GUIDE

COLOR PALETTE

Main panel **Variation**

MOSAIC 27: SEASHELLS

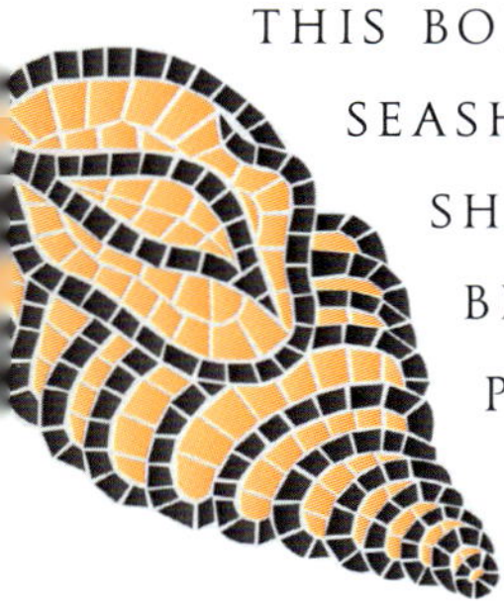

THIS BOLD, STYLIZED DESIGN IS BASED ON THE NATURAL FORM OF SEASHELLS. THE BRIGHT BACKGROUND SQUARES GIVE THE SHELLS A BLEACHED-OUT, CHALKY FEEL. THE DESIGN COULD BE RECONFIGURED AS A FRIEZE OR BORDER. ALTERNATIVELY PLAIN WALL TILES COULD BE INTERSPERSED AT INTERVALS WITH THE MOTIFS CREATED AS SINGLE TILE-SIZED PIECES.

Skill level: **2**

Materials

Standard-size vitreous tiles

Estimating tile quantities, **see page 11**

COLOR PALETTE

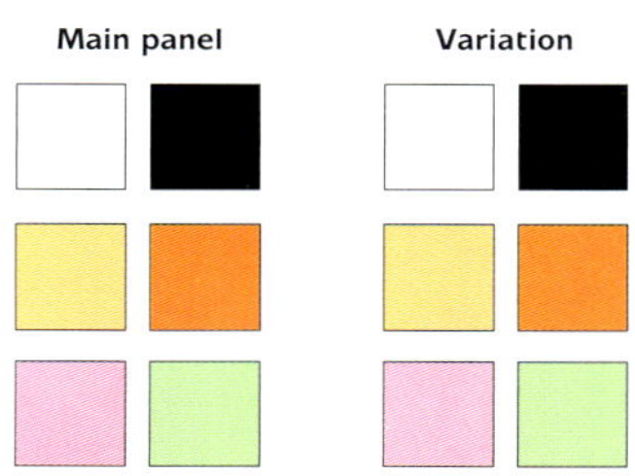

ORDER OF WORK **KEY**

PANEL TRANSFER GRID

Order of work

1 Start with the outline of each of the shells. The idea is to make the strong line look drawn. Take time to ensure that the tiles are of even thickness, and that they are tapered to follow the many curves of the design smoothly.

2 Now move on to the infill of the shells; again strive for evenness with the fills following the curves where possible. Filling "flat" areas like this requires great care, as the tiles must flow together, rather than just be placed in a jumble.

3 The background squares should be completed one at a time so that each is distinct, with a strong "edge." Start with the top left-hand motif, then move left to right and downward.

Suggested dimensions

To scale and transfer the design follow the techniques described on pages 18–19.

Size of design: 25 x 33 in. (63.5 x 84 cm).

TILE CUTTING AND PLACEMENT GUIDE

VARIATION: CARTOON-LIKE

Color variation

This treatment is more cartoon-like, with each shell isolated against a white background. You could recreate the grid of the tiles using sliver-thin pieces of tile of a dark tone to create outlines.

MOSAIC 28: BOBBING BOATS

A SIMPLE BUT STRIKING PIECE SHOWING THAT BOLD, CLEAR DESIGN WITHOUT TOO MUCH DETAIL CAN BE EFFECTIVE. GET THE SOLID FOUNDATION OF THE CURVING WAVES RIGHT AND THE REST OF THE PIECE WILL FALL INTO PLACE. THE CHALLENGE IS THE LINE OF THE CABLE RUNNING BETWEEN THE MASTS; CUT LOTS OF THIN SHARDS OF TILE AND REJECT ANY THAT ARE NOT PERFECTLY MATCHED IN THICKNESS BEFORE YOU BEGIN GLUING THEM DOWN.

ORDER OF WORK **KEY**

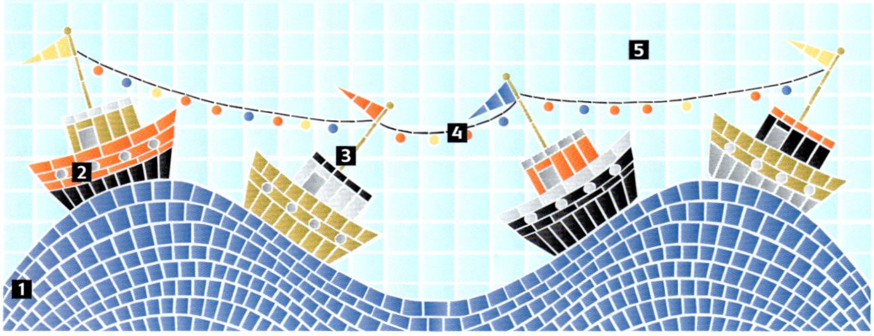

COLOR PALETTE

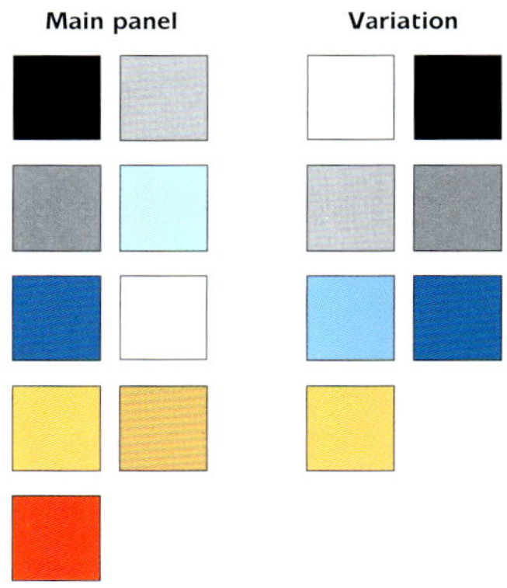

Skill level: **1**

Materials

Standard-size vitreous tiles
Estimating tile quantities, **see page 11**

TILE CUTTING AND PLACEMENT GUIDE

Order of work

1 Start with the waves, laying a line of tiles at a time and ensuring that you taper the edges which butt together so that the tiles follow the lines of the curve.

2 Lay the hulls of each boat, placing them so that they ride the curve of the wave that supports them. Cut small circles of tiles for the portholes first, then lay the bulk of the tiles around these. Simple rectangles make up each of the deckhouses.

3 Use thinly cut tile fragments to make the mast, which is topped with a triangular pennant.

4 The cable of lights joining the boats requires the most care: take time to cut really thin pieces of tiles and ensure that they follow the different loops between the masts accurately. Smaller circular cuts of different colors provide the individual bulbs. Again make sure that they are of equal size.

5 Finish with the sky: you can use a wave-like fill that mimics the curve of the waves or try a flat rectangular fill to give contrast.

PANEL TRANSFER GRID

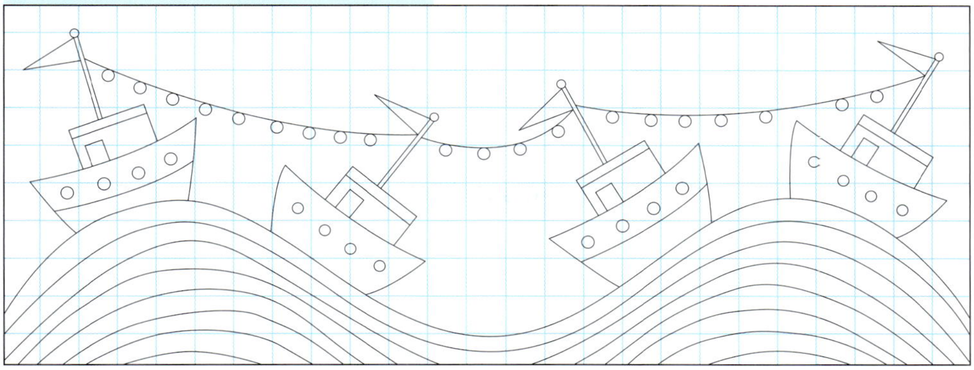

Suggested dimensions

To scale and transfer the design follow the techniques described on pages 18–19. Size of design: 9 x 23½ in. (23 x 59.5 cm).

Color variation

The design works well as a night scene, with the sky darker than the sea below and the bulbs suggesting a cozy, flickering warmth. The individual boats are more subtly colored and closer in tone to give them a ghost-like quality.

VARIATION: NIGHT SCENE

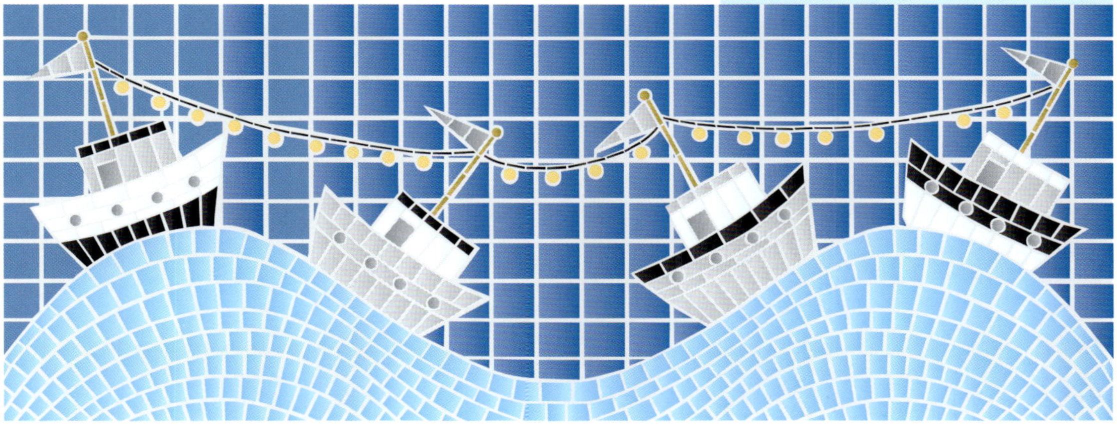

MOSAIC 29:
SUNS AND STARS

THIS PIECE USES HOUSEHOLD CERAMIC TILES, SO THAT EACH OF THE FACES AND LARGE RAYS CAN BE CUT FROM A SINGLE TILE. CUT YOUR CIRCLES AND PAINT ON THE FEATURES IN ADVANCE SO THAT THE CERAMIC PAINTS CAN BE OVEN-FIRED. HOUSEHOLD TILES ARE NOT AS DURABLE AS VITREOUS TILES, SO CHOOSE A LOCATION FOR THIS PIECE WHERE IT WILL NOT BE SUBJECT TO EXCESSIVE MOISTURE OR WEAR.

Skill level: **3**

Materials

Household ceramic tiles with oven-fired ceramic paints
Estimating tile quantities, **see page 11**

COLOR PALETTE

Main panel | Variation

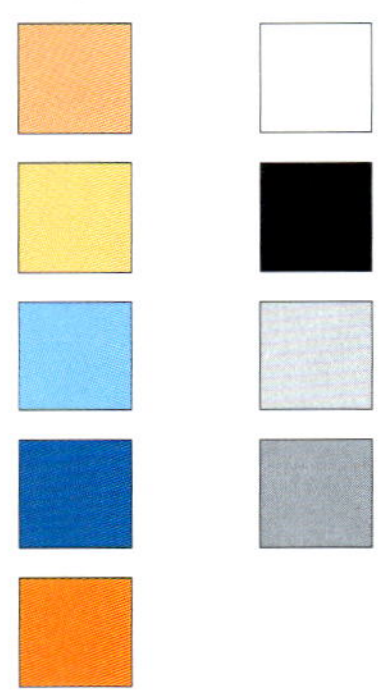

Suggested dimensions

To scale and transfer the design follow the techniques described on pages 18–19.
Size of design: 17¾ x 17¾ in. (45 x 45 cm).

PANEL TRANSFER GRID

ORDER OF WORK **KEY**

Order of work

1 Start by laying the pre-prepared face, then cut appropriately sized rectangles and draw the outlines of the different "rays"—curving the bottom edges so that they fit the circular shape. Fit the outer band of rays to the drawn circle; then fill the whole section with a crackle fill.

2 Cut the pentagonal-shaped central piece of the star, then cut triangles for each arm. Then complete this section with a radial fill.

3 The longer, fine rays of this sun are very challenging to cut as single pieces. When you have laid them, you will then have to produce the same again to provide the fill inbetween—persevere! When complete, surround them with a crackle fill.

4 The same principle as previously but on a smaller scale. The stars work as in the second section—but are smaller. Work outward from the center laying the radial bands, and place your stars when the first band is complete—that way you will have less fiddly cuts to make things fit—try and make the stars occupy the exact width of two bands.

5 These stars are laid at a slight diagonal and then surrounded with a crackle fill.

6 Like the fourth section, but without the stars—the rays in between are cut to have a curvy, softer shape.

7 Long spikes again. Be patient, and nibble away slowly with your nippers,

TILE CUTTING AND PLACEMENT GUIDE

accepting that you will break a few of these fragile shapes along the way. Once again, a crackle pattern fill for the surround.

8 This section is like a simplified version of the first sun, but with an outer surround and radial fill.

9 Just a simple star, again "growing" from a central pentagon and with a crackle background.

VARIATION: MONOCHROME

Color variation
This is a monochrome version using just four tones of gray.

MOSAIC 30: EVENING GOWN

THIS STRIKING FANTAIL DRESS CREATES A VERY FEMININE PIECE. TO MAXIMIZE THE IMPACT OF ITS SHAPE IT IS COMPLETED IN A SINGLE COLOR, WITH THE PATTERN RENDERED IN A SLIGHTLY LIGHTER SECOND TONE. THE STRONG SHAPE OF THE FIGURE IS FURTHER EMPHASIZED BY THE FAN-FILL BACKGROUND WHICH INCREASES THE SENSE OF A MOVIE STAR SURROUNDED BY FLASHLIGHTS.

Skill level: **3**

Materials

Standard-size vitreous tiles
Estimating tile quantities, **see page 11**

COLOR PALETTE

Main panel **Variation**

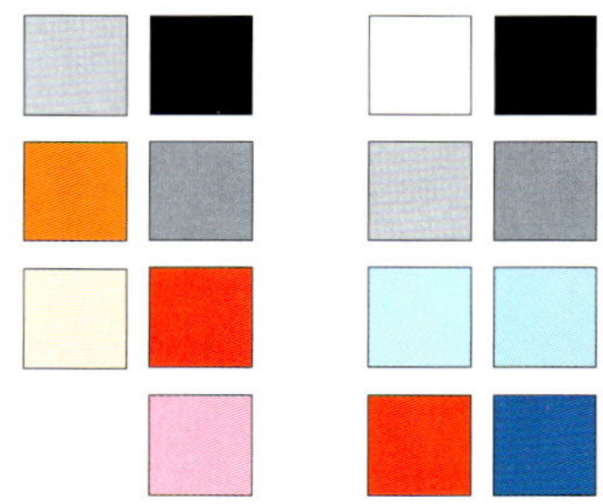

Order of work

1 Start at the top of the figure, tiling the butterfly, surrounding this with the hair, and working down to the kiss-curl over the face. Tile the eyes, eyebrows, and nose with as much precision as you can manage, then the lips. All need to look like smooth, clean brush lines without any kinks in the way they are laid. Fill the flesh tones, working down to the neck. Cut matching pairs of tiles to create each piece of the earrings.

2 Create the beads of the necklace, cutting those at the back so that they seem to disappear behind the neck.

3 Begin the dress with the frill of the bodice, created with looped bands of small tiles. Place the center of each flower, then tile around them with the lighter-toned tiles to create the petals. Next, background fill around the flowers, taking care to keep the flowing outline in the darker color. Finally, use parallel bands of tapering tiles to complete each section of the "fishtail" of the dress. Finish with the trailing evening shawl hanging to the right of the figure.

4 Now go back and tile the shoulders, fitting the tiles carefully around the decorative detail, and flowing them smoothly down the line of the arms.

5 The background fill is drawn using a pair of compasses to create the rows of arches. Start at the bottom, working along a horizontal line to place the first row of semi-circles side-by-side. Draw a line across the top of the first row of arches, then mark the center point on this line between the arches below to place your compasses to create the next row. Continue in this way to the top of the picture, then simply tile inward from each line with bands of tiles, carefully cutting the tiles so that they are tapered to follow the curve.

ORDER OF WORK **KEY**

PANEL TRANSFER GRID

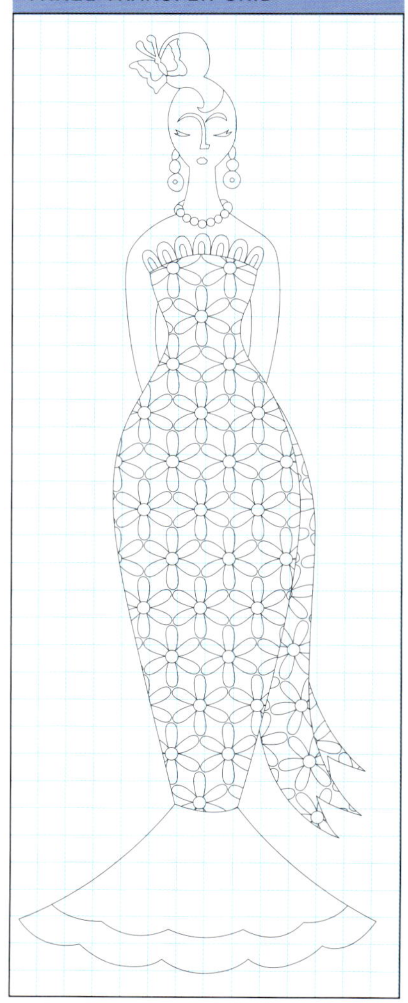

VARIATION: TROPICAL MOONLIGHT

TILE CUTTING AND PLACEMENT GUIDE

Color variation

This blue version has an even stronger retro atmosphere, reminiscent of those popular prints of the 1950s, which showed exotic ladies under tropical moonlight.

Suggested dimensions

To scale and transfer the design follow the techniques described on pages 18–19. Size of design: 35 x 13⅝ in. (89 x 34.5 cm).

MOSAIC 31: FABULOUS FLOWERS

THIS IS AN EXUBERANT, EXAGGERATED DESIGN OF PLUMP, CURVY PLANTS AND SPIKY FOLIAGE. THE BIGGER YOU CAN MAKE IT, THE MORE IMPACT IT WILL HAVE, BUT REMEMBER THAT IT WILL DOMINATE MOST SETTINGS IN THESE HOT, ORANGE AND RED COLORS. HOWEVER, IT IS A RELATIVELY SIMPLE PIECE TO COMPLETE, CONSISTING OF FLAT AREAS OF COLOR.

Skill level: **2**

Materials

Standard-size vitreous tiles or household ceramic tiles
Estimating tile quantities, **see page 11**

ORDER OF WORK **KEY**

Order of work

1 Start with the first of the spear-like leaves, working out from the central core. By working with large tile pieces you can make the design bold, and also cover larger areas quickly.

2 Draw a strong, smooth curve for the central heart-shaped foliage, then fill the heart shapes working upward from the bottom and out from the central line, completing one heart before moving on to the next.

3 The third flower follows the same principle, but finishes with a bursting flower. Here, establish the small, seed shapes then build the bloom around them.

4 Move to the other side of the mosaic and complete the "pod"-shaped plant, again working upward and outward from the central line.

5–8 More spear-like leaves; complete those in the foreground first.

9 Move on to the large flowers, completing those in the foreground first. Do the small shapes first, then fill around them.

10 Next, complete the flowers that are "behind" other parts of the design.

11 The background here has a crackle fill, which can be tricky to do. Alternatively, fill the background space with more regularly cut tiles following the outlines of the flowers, or try a checkerboard fill.

12 The border is optional, but provides a nice finish. Cut simple, thin rectangles from all the colors you have used in the piece.

Color variation

This design could be adapted to almost any color palette. Here, more muted pinks and greens have been combined, suggesting a humid heat rather than the "desert heat" of the first version.

VARIATION: RAINFOREST

TILE CUTTING AND PLACEMENT GUIDE

COLOR PALETTE

Main panel **Variation**

PANEL TRANSFER GRID

Suggested dimensions

To scale and transfer the design follow the techniques described on pages 18–19. Size of design: 16⅜ x 33 in. (41.5 x 84 cm).

MOSAIC 32: HEARTS

THIS STRONG, BOLD DESIGN HAS A SIMPLE BUT STRIKING SHAPE THAT MIGHT WORK WELL IN A TEENAGER'S ROOM. PLACING THE DESIGN ON A WHITE BACKGROUND CREATES A STRIKING POSTER-LIKE QUALITY.

Skill level: **2**

Materials

Standard-size vitreous tiles or ceramic tiles
Estimating tile quantities, **see page 11**

ORDER OF WORK **KEY**

PANEL TRANSFER GRID

Suggested dimensions

To scale and transfer the design follow the techniques described on pages 18–19.
Size of design: 29½ x 30 in. (75 x 76 cm).

Order of work

1–10 This design is deceptive; do not underestimate the work involved. The drawing and the tile cutting need to be absolutely perfect. Start from the center, tackling each concentric heart one at a time. You can simplify the design by reducing the total number of hearts, but however many hearts you decide on and whatever fill you use, make sure that you maintain the symmetry of each one. If you decide on a checkerboard fill, then work from the vertical center-line as you complete each heart to ensure that you maintain the balance between the left and right side of the design.

11–16 Now move on to the background squares. Again, follow the same principles—symmetry and balance are most important. As with the hearts, you can reduce or add to the number of squares.

VARIATION: MONOCHROME

TILE CUTTING AND PLACEMENT GUIDE

COLOR PALETTE

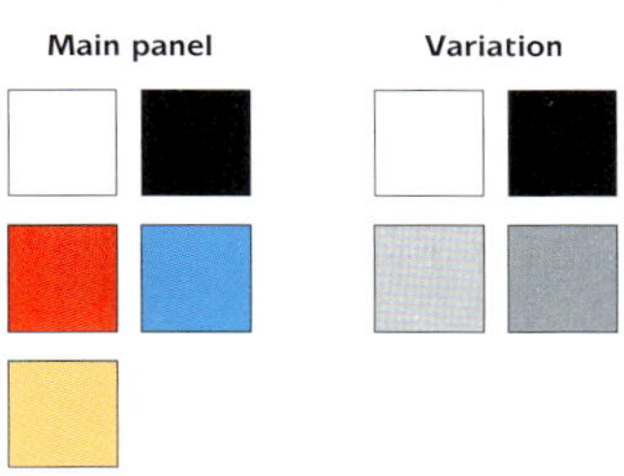

Color variation

As an alternative to the five-color palette, try a monochrome treatment. This is just as dynamic but easier in a setting that does not allow garish colors.

MOSAIC 33: HANDBAGS

A BRIGHT PANEL SUITED TO A TEENAGER'S BEDROOM, A HALLWAY, OR A STORE. THIS IS A SIMPLE AND STYLIZED PIECE WITH A STARTLING COLOR PALETTE THAT YOU CAN ADAPT TO SUIT YOUR TASTE. IT WOULD WORK EQUALLY WELL MASSIVELY ENLARGED ON A WALL, OR SMALLER, PERHAPS PLACED ABOVE A ROW OF COAT HOOKS OR PEGS.

Skill level: **2**

Materials

Standard-size vitreous tiles
Estimating tile quantities, **see page 11**

TILE CUTTING AND PLACEMENT GUIDE

Order of work

1 Start from left to right. The first bag is angular, so accentuate the hard edges and use severe, rectangular cuts. Gold tiles would be ideal for the detail of the buckle.

2 The next one is like a carpet bag. Start with the motif on the right, then use a fill that follows the curves of the outline. Finish with the ring of the handle using accurately laid black tiles to create the effect of a hard plastic or bone-like material.

3 Complete the flower motif of this purse-like bag first, then surround with an outline of tiles of a single, strong color. Again, gold tiles would be good for the clasp.

4 If you are working on a large scale, try and introduce one or two highlight tiles into the bunch of cherries motif. The bulk of the bag can be completed with a simple herringbone or zigzag fill to create the effect of a basket weave.

5 Pre-cut a number of semi-circular tiles and sort them in ascending size to create the spiral patterns. A shocking, vivid background in a contrasting or complementary color works best to surround the spirals.

6 Cut and place the heart first. Again semi-circles provide a lacy edging to this bag which is completed with a solid black fill in both color variations.

7 Use a regular, rectangular fill for the background.

ORDER OF WORK KEY

COLOR PALETTE

Main panel | Variation

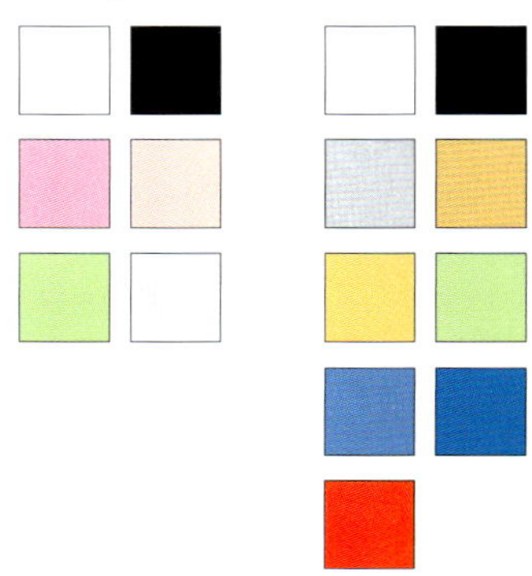

PANEL TRANSFER GRID

Suggested dimensions
To scale and transfer the design follow the techniques described on pages 18–19. Size of design: 9 x 30½ in. (23 x 77.5 cm).

VARIATION: NEUTRAL

Color variation
This more naturalistic color palette, on a neutral background, can be gentler on the eye for some locations.

MOSAIC 34: RUSSIAN DOLLS

THIS DESIGN IS BASED ON THE FAMOUS NESTING OR STACKING DOLLS, KNOWN AS MATRYOSHKI, FROM 19TH-CENTURY RUSSIA. EACH DESIGN IS SUBTLY DIFFERENT WITH VARIATIONS IN THE EYELASHES AND CHEEKS OF THE FACES AND THE DECORATIVE FLOWERS ON THE BODIES. THE BORDER IS A TESSELLATION PATTERN TAKEN FROM TRADITIONAL RUSSIAN FOLK ART.

Skill level: **3**

Materials

Option 1: Standard-size vitreous tiles
Option 2: Ceramic tiles with oven-fired ceramic paints
Estimating tile quantities, **see page 11**

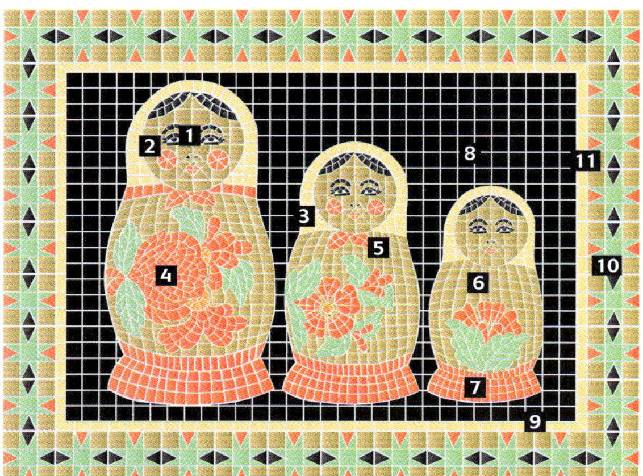

ORDER OF WORK **KEY**

Suggested dimensions
To scale and transfer the design follow the techniques described on pages 18–19. Size of design: 22 x 28¾ in. (56 x 73 cm).

PANEL TRANSFER GRID

Order of work

1 This design is more effective the larger you make it. The delicate detail of the facial features is easier when the design is larger. Place the cheeks, hair, and eyes; make sure that the tiles for the left and right side of each face match in size. Measure carefully from a central line to ensure they are placed symmetrically.

2 Complete the circular outline of the faces, then work inward to fill each one.

3 Now do the headscarves, again cutting accurately to the curve.

4 Start with the central parts of the flower, then cut the petals. Use nibbling techniques to soften the edges and reproduce the hand-painted look of the original dolls.

5 Add the detail of the neckties.

6 Now complete the surrounding shape of the body.

7 Finish each figure with the solid fill of the base.

8 Fill in the large area of the main background patiently, keeping the tiles evenly sized and spaced.

9 Split tiles into long, thin rectangles and carefully lay the inner border.

10 Now place the central tiles of the outer border, placing them precisely on the grid.

11 If you have worked accurately, the border motif is relatively quick to complete as it only requires simple triangular splits of whole tiles to surround each square.

Color variation

This version uses plain ceramic tiles, with the features of the faces painted onto circles, each cut from a single piece of tile. Even if you follow the same color palette, the finished piece will have a very different look when executed in plain tiles.

Variation with ceramic tiles

If completing the piece in ceramic tiles, the order of work is much the same but the techniques are a bit different.

Start by cutting each of the circles for the faces from separate ceramic tiles, then paint the features using oven-fired ceramic paints—you can wipe off any mistakes as long as you do not let the paint dry. When you are happy, fire the painted tile pieces following the instructions supplied with the paint.

Then work on the dolls, the background, and the outer pattern in the same order as described opposite. You may find this variation simpler because you are painting rather than cutting the finer detail; however, the ceramic tiles will have a less vibrant color than their vitreous counterparts. Take care when grouting the tiles as excessive scouring to remove the grout may damage the hand-painted areas.

COLOR PALETTE

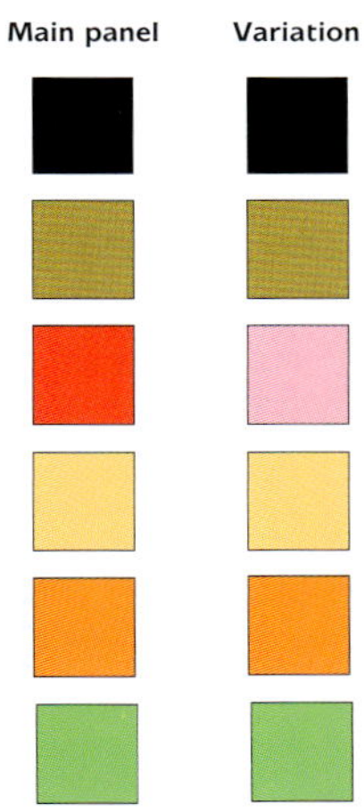

TILE CUTTING AND PLACEMENT GUIDE

MOSAIC 35: ALPHABET

THIS ALPHABET DESIGN IS IDEAL FOR A HALL OR CORRIDOR IN A KINDERGARTEN OR SCHOOL. AS THE DESIGN IS BUSY–USING DIFFERENT TYPEFACES, FILLS, AND BACKGROUND COLORS–TAKE CARE NOT TO MAKE IT TOO CHAOTIC. WITH SO MUCH VARIETY IT IS IMPORTANT TO IMPOSE BALANCE AND ORDER. THIS PIECE REQUIRES VERY CAREFUL PLANNING AND PRECISION CUTTING. LETTERS ARE ELEGANT SHAPES, AND THE SLIGHTEST DEVIATION FROM THE OUTLINE CAN MAKE THEM LOOK "WRONG."

ORDER OF WORK **KEY**

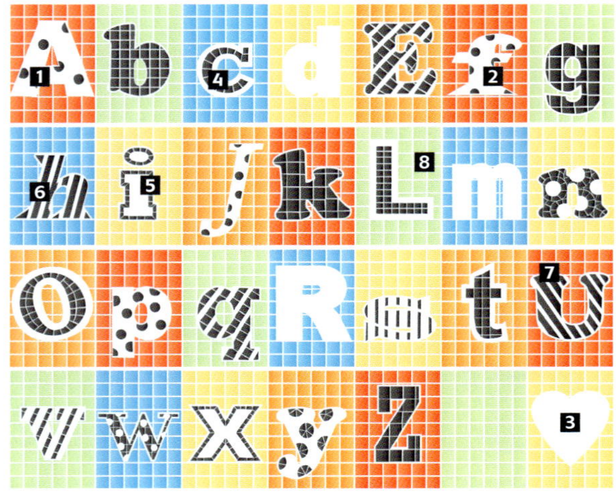

Suggested dimensions
To scale and transfer the design follow the techniques described on pages 18–19. Size of design: 30 x 37½ in. (76 x 95 cm).

Skill level: **3**

Materials

Standard-size vitreous tiles
Estimating tile quantities, **see page 11**

PANEL TRANSFER GRID

Order of work
Different letters that use the same fill should be approached in the same way as follows:

1 For the polka dot fill: first place small circular-cut tiles, trying to keep them evenly spaced, and cutting into them precisely where they go over the edge of the letter.

2 Cut the tiles of the main fill of each letter to fit round the polka dots, then place them. Mark the line of the letter edges with a washable felt-tip pen, then cut them precisely to fit, testing the accuracy of each piece before gluing it down.

3 The solid fill: make sure you cut exactly to the outlines, taking care to ensure that curves are smooth. (When doing the heart, draw a central, vertical line, and work out from each side to make sure your fill is symmetrical.)

4–5 For the outline letters, cut a good supply of narrow strips of tile, ensuring they are exactly the same thickness, then tile round the outline. You will find you have to break the strips into very small pieces to get the tight curves of the hooks and serifs on some letters. Let the glued down outlines set, then carefully cut the fill. Make sure you leave even spaces for grout—don't cram the inside of the letter too tightly.

6–7 For the stripes, always begin with the narrow bands then tile the fill in between. Again, your drawing

TILE CUTTING AND PLACEMENT GUIDE

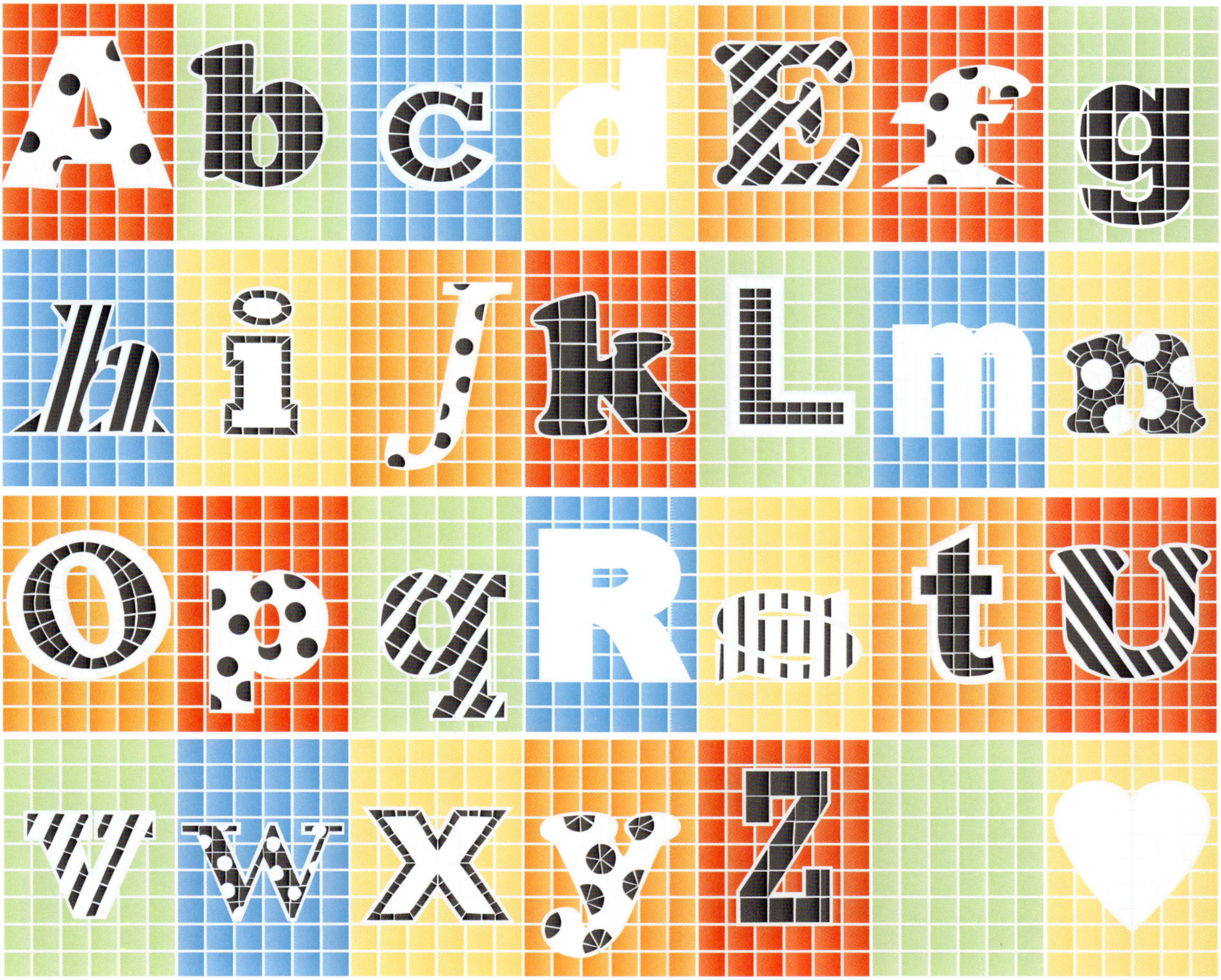

preparation is important so that the stripes are equally spaced in relation to the edges of the letter.

8 Finish with the background fill for each letter "tile," alternating the colors in order. The blank tile between the Z and the heart is a "spacer" to make the number of panels on each row the same. You could fill this with a flower, school logo, or other motif.

Color variation

This variation uses a stark black and white background with just two fill colors.

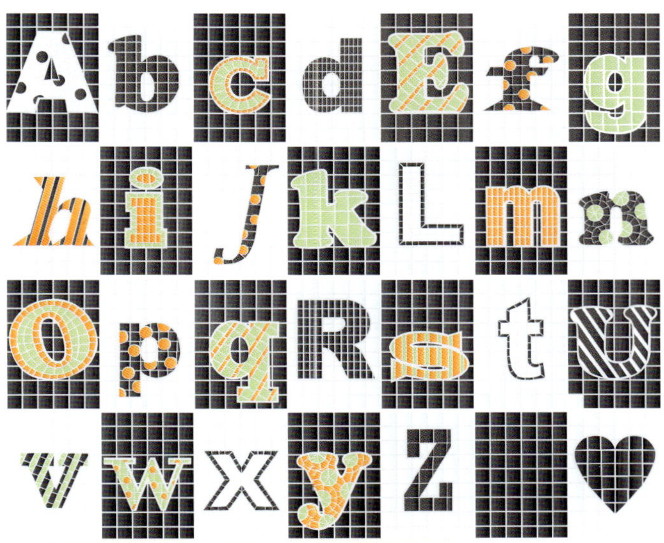

VARIATION: STARK

COLOR PALETTE

MOSAIC 36: JUNGLE

THIS PICTURE HAS A CHILD-LIKE QUALITY, FRESH AND BRIGHT, BUT QUITE REALISTIC. THE PIECE UTILIZES DIFFERENT MATERIALS BUT RELIES CHIEFLY ON HOUSEHOLD CERAMIC TILES. THE COMPARATIVE SOFTNESS OF THIS TYPE ALLOWS YOU TO CUT BIG PIECES WITH A LOT OF ACCURACY AND CURVES THAT FLOW BOTH INWARD AND OUTWARD. THE PICTURE USES "CHUNKY" COLORS AND DESIGN BUT ALSO CREATES STRONG ANIMAL CHARACTERS.

Skill level: **3**

Materials

Household ceramic tiles, "millefiori" tiles (tiny slices of colored Italian glass that can be obtained from specialist craft suppliers), pebbles
Estimating tile quantities, **see page 11**

Suggested dimensions

To scale and transfer the design follow the techniques described on pages 18–19. Size of design: 19 x 19 in. (48 x 48 cm).

PANEL TRANSFER GRID

ORDER OF WORK **KEY**

Order of work

1 Start with the sun by drawing round a suitably sized circular shape on a ceramic tile with a felt-tip pen. Cut the circle and position it, then create the rays from thin rectangular cuts. Use a protractor to mark out their position. Each outer point will be at a 45-degree interval; the angle which touches the inner circle is half-way between. Curve the base of each "ray" to fit the central circle.

2 Draw paper templates for the sections of the tree trunk, getting progressively smaller, then trace each onto tile rectangles before cutting them out. Then move on to the palm leaves—using the finished side of a tile for all the framing edges of the picture.

3 The monkey is not just a silhouette—follow the cuts carefully so that the grout lines suggest the two back legs. Dovetail the pieces of the tail to give it a smooth curve.

4 Start with the body of the butterflies. Using ceramic tiles allows you to cut large slabs of bright color to complete each section of wing in one piece.

5 Next is the palm tree; this needs careful positioning of the tile pieces to create the smooth curves. Place the leaves, cut small rectangles in two different tones of the same color and then curve one side. Pair these shapes together to create the whole leaf.

6 The flowers have a center of millefiori tiles. Surround each center with petals but don't make them overly perfect; in this case variation in size and shape adds interest.

7 Place the small pebble beach. Find pebbles that are flat and as evenly shaped as possible. The shard-shaped leaves ground the design; and working with a paper template helps. Cut some leaves in different colors, then split and alternate the pieces to create a banded effect.

COLOR PALETTE

Main panel | Variation

TILE CUTTING AND PLACEMENT GUIDE

8 The lion provides a key personality in the design. Place eyes, nose, and other facial details first, concentrating on spacing everything symmetrically. Accentuate the shapes, particularly the wide eyes.

9 Crackle fill the elephant to give an impression of creased skin. You could stick on a "googly" eye—available from craft stores—after the piece has been grouted. The elephant's tusk can be cut from one piece of tile.

10 The cloud is a contour fill that winds around the sun.

11 The background is laid in toned vertical bands to give a sense of depth to the picture.

VARIATION: STYLIZED

Color variation

You could use a palette of "hot" colors, which, combined with the black background, creates a highly stylized result.

MOSAIC 37: BIG TOP

THIS DRAMATIC DESIGN HAS THE "RETRO" FEELING OF A 1950s ILLUSTRATION. IT USES EXAGGERATED SHADOWS AND HIGHLIGHTS, LIKE ON THE TOP HAT OF THE DASHING RINGMASTER. THE DESIGN IS IN THE SHAPE OF A CIRCUS BIG TOP CUT FROM MDF. THE STARS CREATE ADDITIONAL COLOR AND NOISE, LIKE FIREWORKS OR FLASHBULBS BURSTING OUT OF THE MORE MUTED BACKGROUND.

VARIATION: REVERSAL

Skill level: **3**

Materials

Standard-size vitreous tiles
Estimating tile quantities, **see page 11**

PANEL TRANSFER GRID

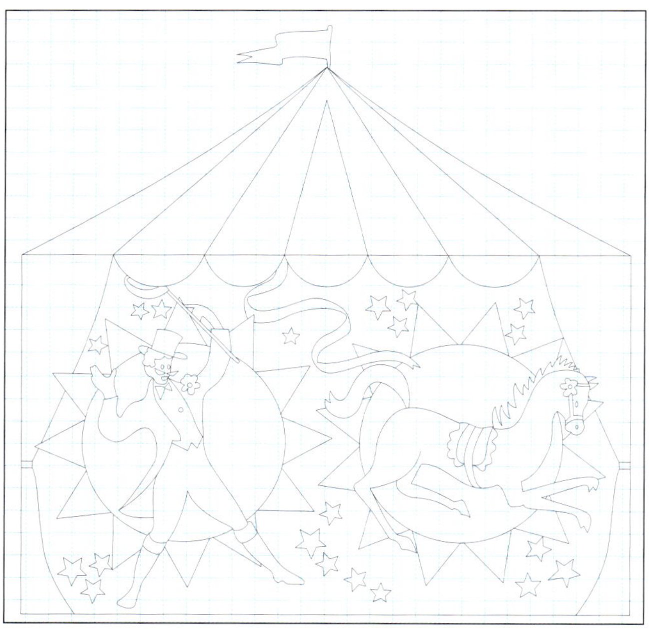

Suggested dimensions

To scale and transfer the design follow the techniques described on pages 18–19.
Size of design: 35¼ x 37 in. (89.5 x 94 cm).

COLOR PALETTE

Main panel | Variation

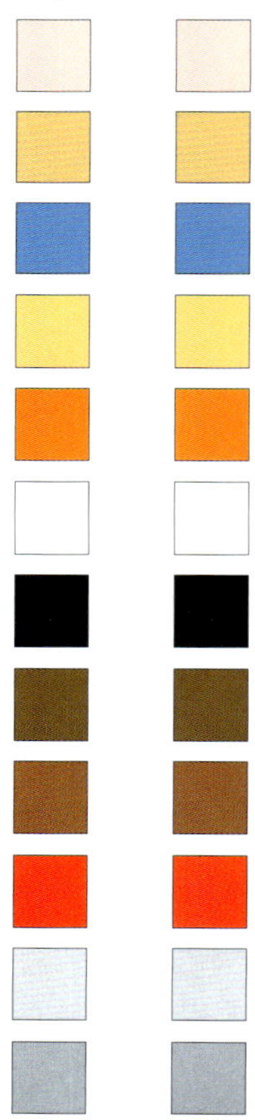

Color variations

This alternative palette is almost a "reversal" of the first version, with the background turned into a much stronger element. If you choose this variation, consider the surrounding colors where the finished piece will be placed as such a strong area of red may clash with some color schemes.

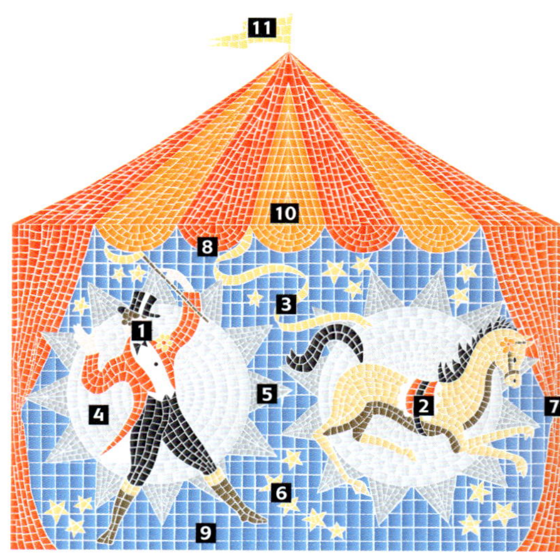

ORDER OF WORK **KEY**

TILE CUTTING AND PLACEMENT GUIDE

Order of work

1 Begin with the ringmaster, establishing the details of the face and the highlight of his top hat. Pay attention to his hands holding the baton.

2 Complete the saddle and bridle of the horse first. Exaggerate the curves of the horse's back and give it depth by adding shading to the underside of the body.

3 Tile the ringmaster's baton and ribbon, working carefully to make the ribbon shape across the picture.

4 Make the circular shapes out of concentric rings of tiles.

5 The triangles require careful tapering to give them "sharpness."

6 Work precisely to make the stars look as if they have been spread about casually.

7 The drapes frame the piece; pay attention to the detail of the pleats.

8 Make the fringe of the canopy from semi-circles.

9 Fill in the interior background around the stars and other detail.

10 The canopy requires patience to both recede and keep the symmetry of the design.

11 You can personalize the design by placing an initial or other motif in the flag.

MOSAIC 38: LITTLE PRINCESS

A PORTRAIT OF A FAIRY-TALE PRINCESS. THIS MOSAIC IS OBVIOUSLY MOST SUITABLE FOR A LITTLE GIRL'S BEDROOM. THIS VERSION HAS QUITE NATURALISTIC FLESH TONES AND HAIR COLOR. YOU COULD ADD A FRAME TO THE PIECE, EITHER USING GOLD TILES TO CREATE A PICTORIAL MOSAIC ONE, OR BY HANGING AN OLD PICTURE FRAME AROUND THE PIECE WHEN IT IS IN PLACE ON THE WALL.

Skill level: **3**

Materials

Standard-size vitreous tiles
Estimating tile quantities, **see page 11**

PANEL TRANSFER GRID

Order of work

1–5 The face is the hardest part of this picture. To get balance and symmetry work on the left and right sides together, making sure each piece of tile matches its opposite number as closely as possible. Start with the circles of the cheeks, then move on to the mouth using lots of little cuts to give a soft, curved shape to each tile. The pupils of the eyes have a little cut-out highlight—notice how these are on the same side of the pupil (not opposite sides). Try and cut the lashes into tapering triangular shapes. The main area of the face is filled downward with parallel lines of cut tiles that taper toward the chin. Notice, however the contouring underneath the eyebrows and on the chin itself where the tiles give shape to the features of the face.

6 Carry on down the neck in the same way as the face, pausing at the necklace.

7 Lay the beads of the necklace and decorative pendant, then continue on down the neck trying to follow the same line as above the necklace. End the tiles as exactly as possible on the line of your drawing that establishes the neckline of the dress.

ORDER OF WORK **KEY**

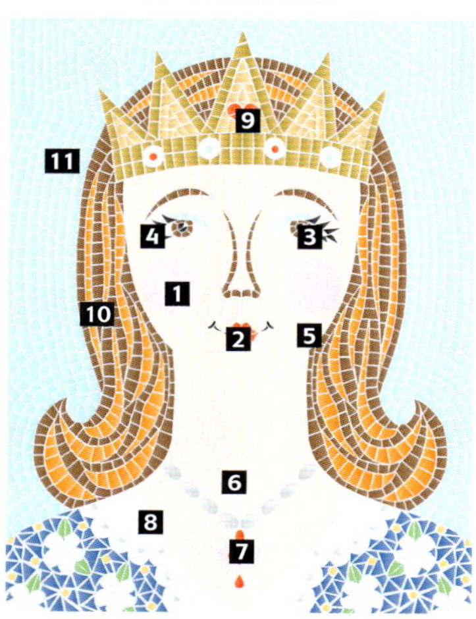

8 Do the scoops of the collar around the neck, then the little scalloped details. The flowers are next: circles surrounded by "clipped" circles, and pairs of split and shaped tiles for each of the leaves. Place the polka dots, then finish the background color of the dress with a crackle fill.

9 The jewels and heart on the crown are next: again, symmetry in placing and sizing is vital. Complete the headband and then the bands surrounding each of the spikes, before filling the inner areas of these with a crackle fill.

10 Do the highlighted areas of the hair first, keeping all the curves nice and soft, then the fill in between with the darker color.

11 The background fill follows the outline of the head to give a slight aura to the picture. At this stage you could add glass jewels and droplets on top of the surface of the finished piece—you may even be able to obtain glass hearts and other suitable shapes from your local craft store.

VARIATION: MAGICAL

Color variation

This variant is more magical with brighter, more vivid pinks and a porcelain skin color.

TILE CUTTING AND PLACEMENT GUIDE

Suggested dimensions

To scale and transfer the design follow the techniques described on pages 18–19. Size of design: 23¼ x 16½ in. (59 x 42 cm).

COLOR PALETTE

Main panel | Variation

MOSAIC 39: NOAH'S ARK

IF YOU HAVE ACCESS TO A JIGSAW, CUT OUT THE OUTLINE SHAPE OF THE BOARD BEFORE LAYING YOUR TILES. OTHERWISE, USE A SIMPLE, WHITE FILL TO THE EDGES OF A CONTAINING RECTANGLE. THIS INTERPRETATION OF THE TRADITIONAL STORY OF THE ARK FEATURES SOME HUMBLER ANIMALS. CAN YOU SPOT BOTH ZEBRAS?

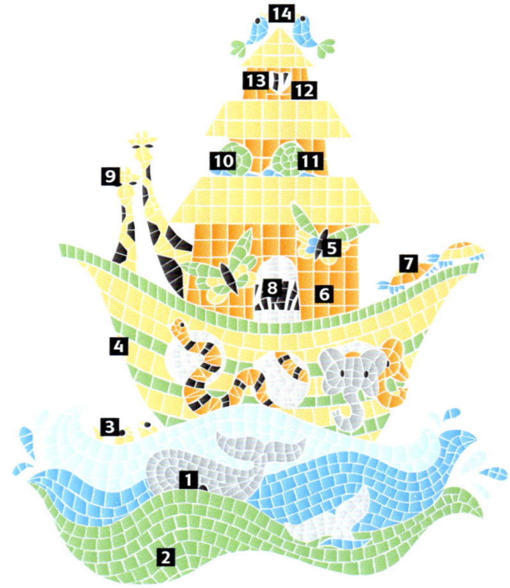

ORDER OF WORK **KEY**

Skill level: **2**

Materials

Standard-size vitreous tiles or household ceramic tiles
Estimating tile quantities, **see page 11**

PANEL TRANSFER GRID

Order of work

1 This project starts from the bottom and works its way up. Begin with the whales, and, as usual, do the eyes first.

2 The fill of the waves should be curvaceous and full.

3 Next, do the two little fish, peeping out from the waves, then the two snakes and the elephants that are in front of the boat.

4 Lay the planks of the ark in parallel rows.

5 Accentuate the shape of the butterflies; keep them large and bright.

6 Establish the first story of the ark, following a simple checkerboard to give some solid areas to anchor what is a "busy" design.

7 Begin with the shells of the two tortoises on the stern, starting from the top and working down before completing the head and feet.

8 Take great care with the zebra stripes because there is little space to balance the white and black areas evenly.

9 The giraffes are exaggerated; accentuate the curve of the neck and the large eyes to give them an aloofness.

10 Coil the snail shells outward from the center, then complete their bodies with a few simple tiles.

11–12 Make the second story, then place the third on top using the same "solid" fill.

Suggested dimensions

To scale and transfer the design follow the techniques described on pages 18–19.
Size of design: 27½ x 22½ in. (70 x 57 cm).

COLOR PALETTE

Main panel | Variation

TILE CUTTING AND PLACEMENT GUIDE

13 Another tricky zebra challenge—this time even finer detail is required.

14 Top the design with two songbirds. You could give the birds (and some of the other animals) "googly eyes"—this is achieved by sticking the eyes on to the mosaic after it has been grouted.

Color variation

Try using a more naturalistic selection of colors: soft blues, mossy greens, and warm browns.

VARIATION: NATURALISTIC

MOSAIC 40: TEDDY BEARS' PICNIC

THIS IS A CHEERFUL PANEL FOR A TODDLER'S ROOM WITH PLENTY OF INTERESTING DETAIL FOR LITTLE EYES, SUCH AS THE DRIPPING ICE CREAM AND THE BUZZING BEES. THERE IS ALSO A COUNTING GAME HIDDEN IN THE DESIGN WITH ONE LOLLIPOP, TWO PRESENTS, THREE VEST BUTTONS, FOUR BALLOONS, FIVE CANDLES, AND SIX SPOTS ON THE TEDDY'S HAT FOR A CHILD TO FIND.

Skill level: **2**

Materials

Standard-size vitreous tiles
Estimating tile quantities, **see page 11**

ORDER OF WORK **KEY**

COLOR PALETTE

Order of work

1 Complete the detail of all the faces first.

2 Move to the foreground areas: tile the presents, paying attention to the ribbon; you can add shading to give a 3-D effect.

3 Start with the candles and then the frosting of the cake.

4 Go back to the first bear and complete the other details: the dots on the hat, then the striped T-shirt, finishing with the ice cream before tiling the body.

5 Move on to the next bear: start with the hat (flowers first), then work down completing the bow. Again, to give a 3-D quality, use a darker color in the folds of the bow.

6 Again start with the party hat before establishing the shape of the vest and filling in the body.

7 Once more take care with the hat, then complete the leotard. Emphasize the "roundness" of the bears by following their outline as you tile them.

8 Move on to the balloons: start with the foremost first and accentuate the highlights. The strings require precision cutting—persevere to get them as thin as you possibly can.

9 Now complete the background flowers.

10 Start with the body of the bees, completing alternate rows of stripes, then work on the wings and tiny antennae.

11 To add contrast, mix different tones of the same color in the background fill.

TILE CUTTING AND PLACEMENT GUIDE

VARIATION: HOT PALETTE

Color variation

The same palette of tiles but with the areas of color swapped around to give a "hotter" end result.

Suggested dimensions

To scale and transfer the design follow the techniques described on pages 18–19. Size of design: 17 x 29⅜ in. (43 x 74.5 cm).

PANEL TRANSFER GRID

12 The sky can be tiled in one color, but you could add clouds or a smiling sun.

13 The frame is an optional addition to provide interest. If you prefer, you could extend the background areas out to the edge of the piece.

MOSAIC 41: HOLDING HANDS

A SIMPLE PIECE USING CERAMIC TILES AND "FOUND OBJECTS," SUCH AS OLD PLATES AND SAUCERS. TAKE IDEAS FROM THE EXAMPLES SHOWN, BUT YOU WILL NEED TO ADAPT THE DESIGNS AND COLORS TO THE PIECES OF TILE AND POTTERY AVAILABLE. YOU CAN ALSO MAKE YOUR OWN "PATTERNED" TILES BY PAINTING PLAIN TILES WITH CERAMIC PAINT.

ORDER OF WORK **KEY**

Skill level: **2**

Materials

Household ceramic tiles, crockery, patterned tiles, oven-fired ceramic paints
Estimating tile quantities, **see page 11**

COLOR PALETTE

Main panel **Variation**

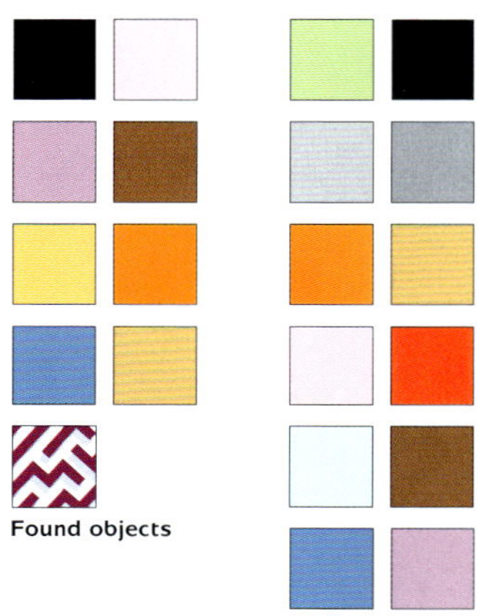

Found objects

Order of work

Before you begin, create faces following the instructions for the Russian Dolls mural on page 93. Prepare them a day or two in advance so that the ceramic inks can be properly cured and dried.

1 Begin with the torso of each figure, placing the triangular tiles. When mixing different ceramic materials, pad out the thinner ones with bits of glue-soaked cardboard to achieve a level surface to the tiles.

2 Move on to the skirt or pants below the torso. To give shape to the skirts, use thin triangular cuts of tiles with the top angle cut off square. If using old bits of china, select pieces that contain interesting pieces of the original pattern.

3–4 To create the arms of the figures, first cut a thin rectangle, then use nippers to nibble along a

TILE CUTTING AND PLACEMENT GUIDE

VARIATION: FLAT COLOR

drawn line from one corner to the center of the opposite, shortest side. Repeat again to create a long thin triangle. Taper the end that butts onto the body so that there is an even grout line.

5 Repeat the same cuts for the legs. Play around with the positioning to create variety and the suggestion of dancing figures.

6 Now place the heads and create different "hair-dos" with simple semi-circles.

7 The hearts are created from two, symmetrically cut, large pieces of tile. Draw the outline with a washable felt-tip pen first.

8 The flowers are a small tile piece cut into a circle, then surrounded with a "dovetailed" band of tapered tiles, then surrounded with a band of petals created from sem -circles of tile.

9 Make the small cats from simple triangles, following the drawing closely.

10 The shapes of the background tiles follows the shape of the characters. Alternatively, you could use a crackle fill.

Color variation

This alternative uses plain ceramic tiles in bright colors which avoids the problem of combining found materials of different thicknesses which can prove difficult to lay evenly.

PANEL TRANSFER GRID

Suggested dimensions

To scale and transfer the design follow the techniques described on pages 18–19. Size of design: 5⅛ x 19½ in. (13 x 49.5 cm).

MOSAIC 42: FISH GAZING

ALTHOUGH THE UNDULATING WEEDS AND WAVES MAKE THIS COMPOSITION RATHER BUSY, THE VIBRANT COLORS OF THE FISH STOP THEM FROM BEING PUSHED INTO THE BACKGROUND. YOU CAN CUT OUT THE PORTHOLE OUTLINE FROM MEDIUM-DENSITY FIBERBOARD USING A JIGSAW.

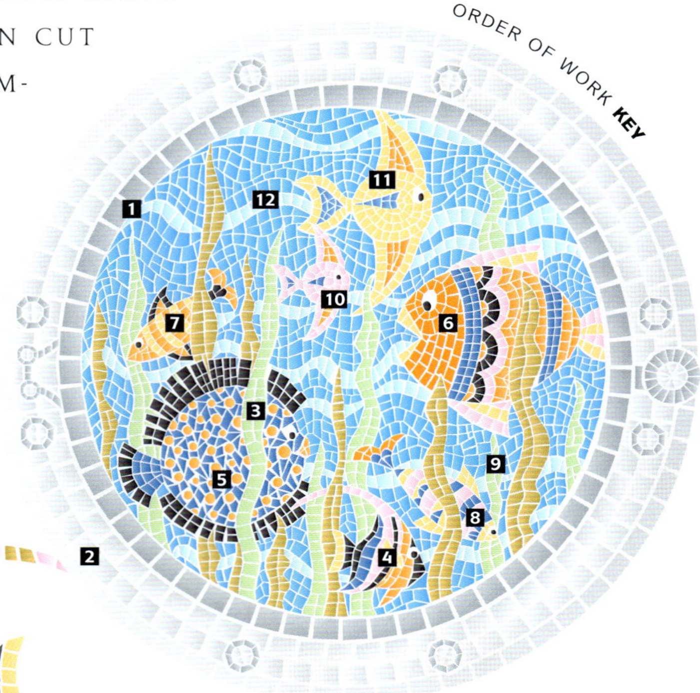

Skill level: **2**

Materials

Standard-size vitreous tiles
Estimating title quantities, **see page 11**

Order of work

1 Begin with the inner rim of the porthole to establish a strong circle.

2 Move to the outer area of the porthole surround, completing all the bolts first.

3 Do the vertical strands of seaweed in the foreground, but leave those fronds which the swimming fish will partly mask until later.

4–8 Work on the fish in order, placing the eye and fine detail, then tiling the smaller stripes and patterns, before filling the larger areas of color.

9 Now complete the background fronds of seaweed, working carefully to fit the tiles around the fish you have just added.

10–11 The last two fish can now be tiled, the one in the foreground first.

12 Finally, complete the background: create a sense of motion, either with wave forms in different tones or with a wavy fill of tiles of the same color.

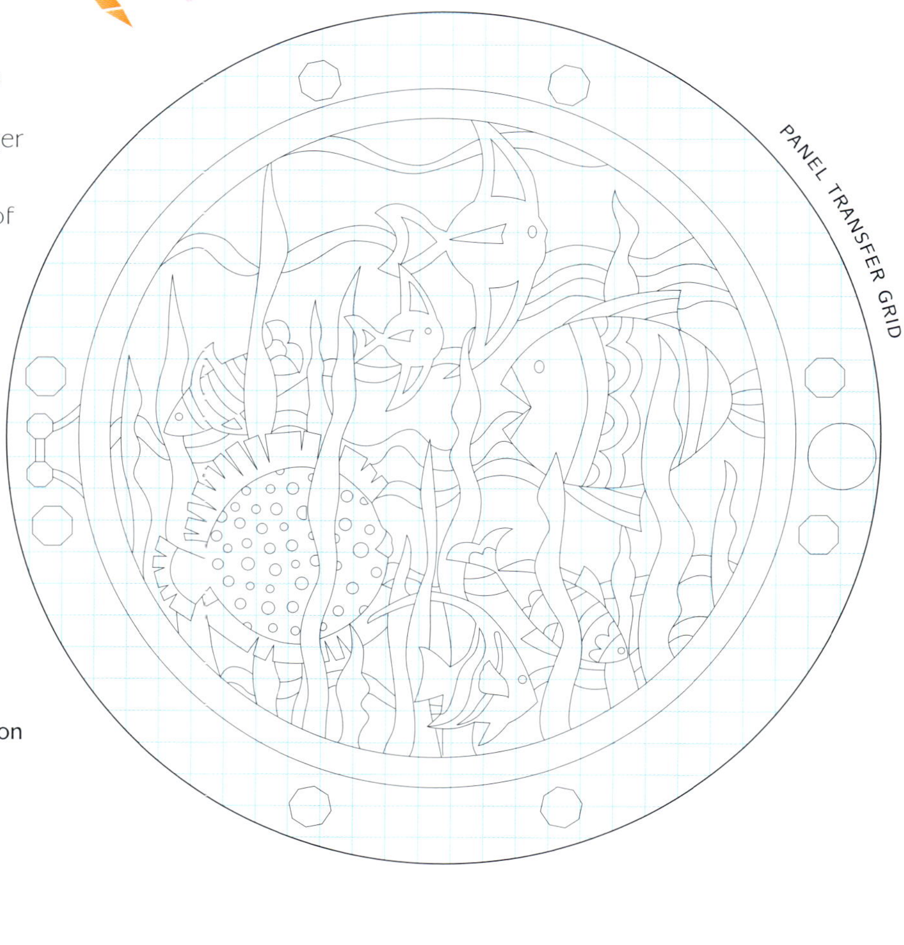

Suggested dimensions

To scale and transfer the design follow the techniques described on pages 18–19. Size of design (diameter): 26⅜ in. (67 cm).

TILE CUTTING AND PLACEMENT GUIDE

VARIATION: HOT PALETTE

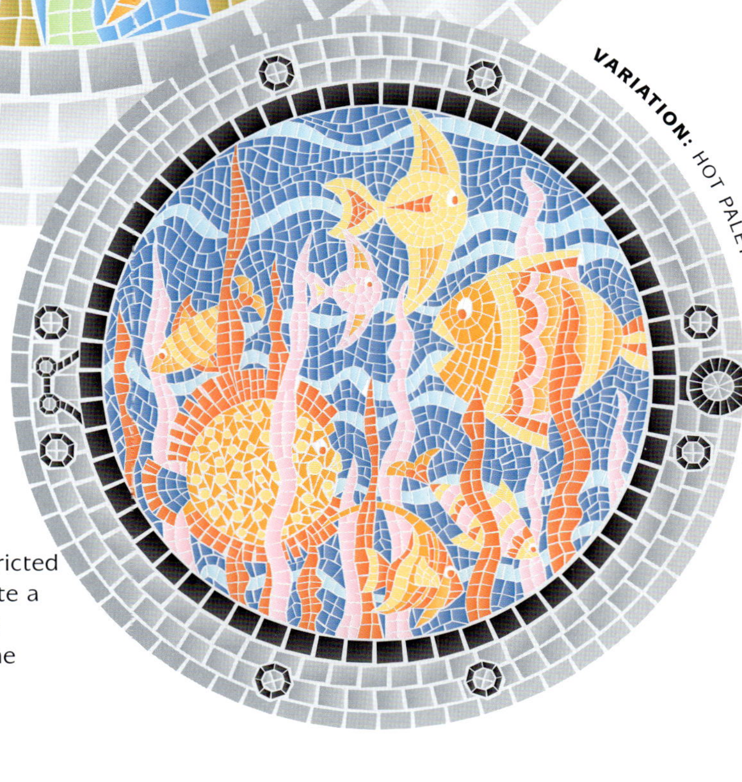

COLOR PALETTE

Color variation

You could use a more restricted set of "hot" colors to create a highly stylized result, even adding "googly" eyes to the fish to give a comic feel.

MOSAIC 43: FARMYARD SCENE

THE GINGHAM BORDERS ON THIS PIECE LEND IT AN "APPLE PIE" AMBIENCE. IT IS SIMPLE TO DO, USING FULL TILES AND JUST THREE COLOR TONES. FOR A CHILD'S ROOM YOU COULD ADD THEIR INITIAL ON THE TRACTOR, OR THEIR ENTIRE NAME ON THE BALES OF HAY LIKE BUILDING BLOCKS. THIS WORKS EQUALLY WELL IN A KITCHEN, PARTICULARLY WITH THIS "FRUITY" COLOR PALETTE.

Skill level: **2**

Materials

Standard-size vitreous tiles
Estimating tile quantities, **see page 11**

ORDER OF WORK **KEY**

Order of work

1 Begin with the tractor wheels, working out from the center, and follow the detail of the tread. Move on to the tractor body.

2 For the dog use lots of fine "nibbling" cuts to give the roundness of the spots, and take care with the details of the eyes before completing the body.

3 Carefully place the stripes and wings of the bee.

4 Now for the bales of hay: integrate any letters that you want in the drawing, and cut carefully around the bee.

5 Place the rooster on top of the tractor roof, working down from the comb to give the flow of the body.

6 Repeat for the hen on the hay bales. Try to make the two chickens look as if they are talking to each other.

7 Pre-cut the center and the surrounding petals of each flower, and experiment with their placement before sticking them down. They need to be accurately sized, so that they recede and each flower is symmetrical.

8 The sun is bold and spiky. Lay the center first, then work out to each ray.

9–10 Fill the background: the strong band of the earth, and the flat area of the sky. You can try different colors.

11 Now the gingham pattern, which, if you use whole tiles, is relatively easy and quick to complete.

PANEL TRANSFER GRID

Suggested dimensions

To scale and transfer the design follow the techniques described on pages 18–19.
Size of design: 21⅝ x 29⅜ in. (55 x 74.5 cm).

TILE CUTTING AND PLACEMENT GUIDE

VARIATION: WARM AND BRIGHT

COLOR PALETTE

Color variation

The gingham has been changed to pinks and reds to give a warmer but still bright end result.

VARIATION: TECHNICOLOR

Suggested dimensions
To scale and transfer the design follow the techniques described on pages 18–19. Size of design: 16½ x 46¾ in. (42 x 118.5 cm).

PANEL TRANSFER GRID

MOSAIC 44: ROLLING TRAIN

THIS IS A SIMPLE PICTORIAL PIECE BECAUSE THE SCALE OF THE ANIMALS AND PLANTS IS NOT CRUCIAL. THE KEY ELEMENT IS THE ROLLER-COASTER FEEL OF THE TRAIN, WHICH YOU CAN ACHIEVE BY LAYING TILES ALONG THE CURVES OF THE HILLS. THE DESIGN HAS A LOVELY PANORAMIC FEEL, WHICH COULD BE EXTENDED RIGHT ALONG A WALL. THE COLOR PALETTE USED HERE FEATURES "NATURAL" COLORS.

Skill level: **2**

Materials

Standard-size vitreous tiles
Estimating tile quantities, **see page 11**

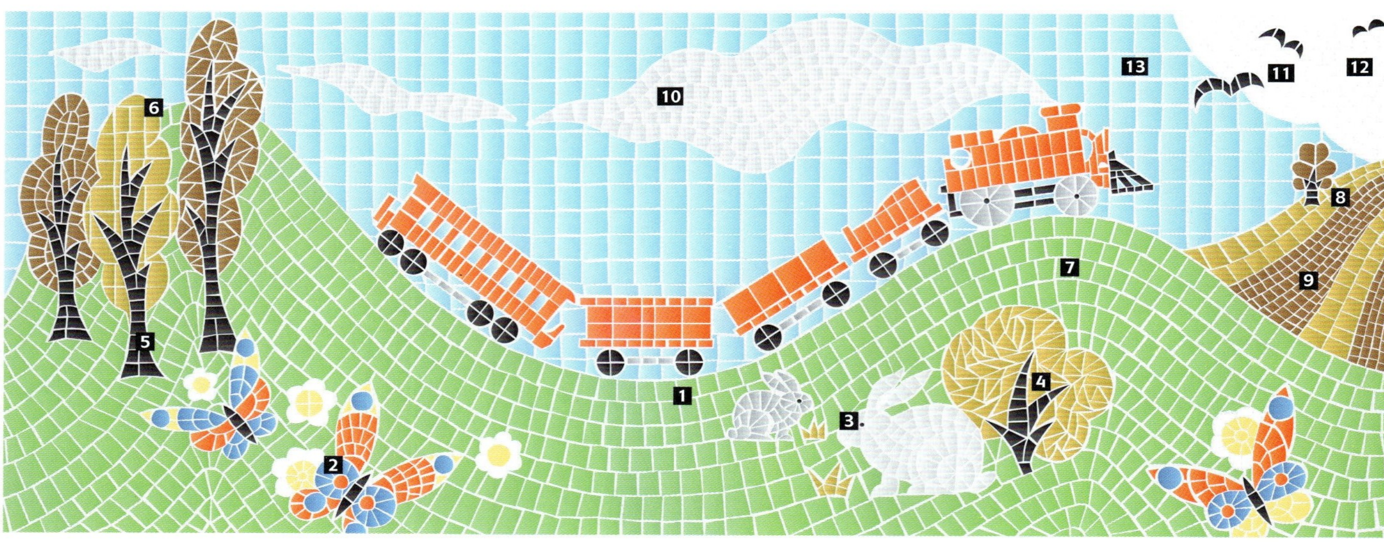

ORDER OF WORK **KEY**

Order of work

1 Start with the centerpiece: draw a strong pencil line for the hills and place the train accurately along it.

2 Place the butterflies and flowers in the foreground.

3 Next do the rabbits; these are kept simple with the only detail being their eyes.

4 Place the bush behind the rabbit, starting with the trunk, then complete the foliage around it.

5–6 As with the bush, do the trunks of the trees first (starting with the center one) then the leaves.

7 Fill in the hill. Your fill should follow the curve of the hills in parallel "ribbons" of the same color.

8 Next, fill the small tree in the background—the picture's focal point.

9 Alternate stripes provide interest and a sense of recession to the field in the background.

10 Accentuate the billowing smoke clouds by following the outline curves with your fill.

11 Render the birds with shards of black tile.

12–13 Surround the birds with the cloud, before filling in the sky.

TILE CUTTING AND PLACEMENT GUIDE

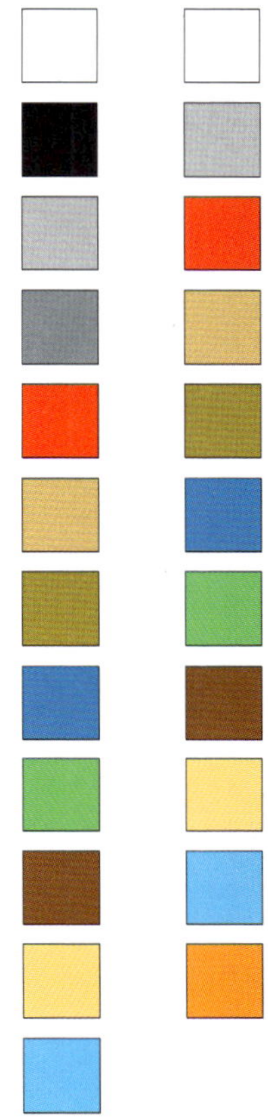

Color variation
This variation is more fanciful, and uses a more technicolor palette of bright, primary colors in a cartoonish way.

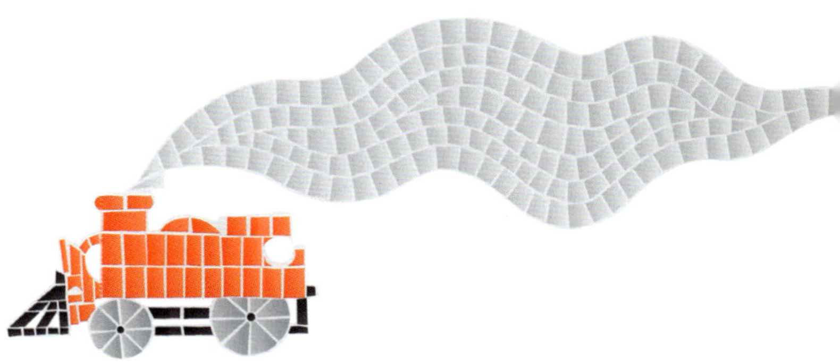

MOSAIC 45: DRAGON

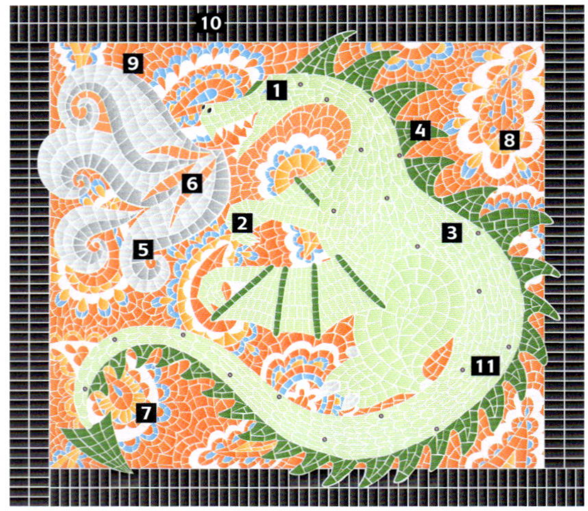

ORDER OF WORK **KEY**

THIS FIERY DRAGON IS MORE A MYTHOLOGICAL BEAST THAN A CUTE DISNEY CREATURE. COMPLEMENTARY COLORS MAKE THE GREEN VERY LUMINOUS, WHILE THE PAISLEY PATTERN BACKGROUND ADDS TO THE EXOTIC FEEL. ADD DIAMANTÉ HIGHLIGHTS TO MAKE THE PICTURE REALLY FLASH AND SPARKLE.

Skill level: **3**

Materials

Vitreous tiles and diamanté decoration
Estimating tile quantities, **see page 11**

Suggested dimensions

To scale and transfer the design follow the techniques described on pages 18–19.
Size of design: 20¼ x 22⅝ in. (51.5 x 57.5 cm).

PANEL TRANSFER GRID

Order of work

1 Start the dragon: create the glinting eye with precisely cut shards of tile, then place the teeth and nostrils.

2 Now tile the arms, wings, and legs. Spend time on the details of the hands and wings to get a spiky, claw-like feel.

3 The bulk of the body has scales; work from the top to create the sense of them overlapping. Curve both the bottom and tops of the tiles so that they fit together with an even space left for grouting.

4 Finish the dragon by tiling the crest along the back; again, start at the head. However you choose to fill this area, make sure the same fill is applied consistently.

5–6 Place the hot flames of the dragon's breath, then the curls of smoke.

7–8 Now begin the paisley pattern of the background, starting with each center. The semicircular details require tight dovetailing to give a smooth effect.

9 Fill in the remaining, plain background areas.

10 The frame surround is optional; if you choose not to include it, then extend the background pattern outward to cover this area.

11 When grouted, add tiny, diamanté details to highlight the dragon's eye and body.

VARIATION: INTENSE

Color variation

Using black for the background strengthens the green, but adds a more mysterious intensity.

COLOR PALETTE

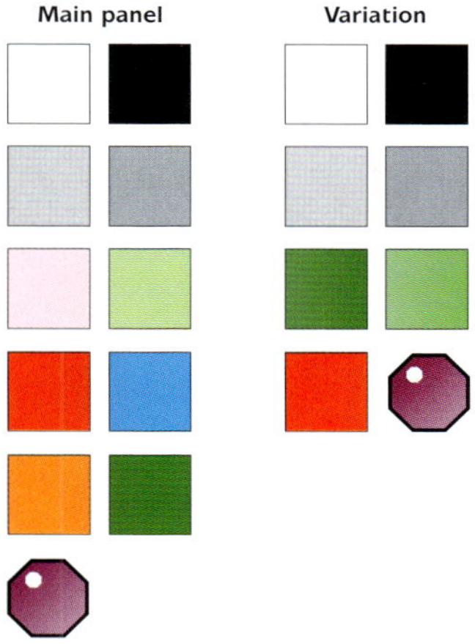

TILE CUTTING AND PLACEMENT GUIDE

MOSAIC 46: TUMBLING DUCKS

A BUSY DESIGN, IDEAL FOR THE NURSERY OR CHILDREN'S BEDROOM, WITH A CAST OF LOVABLE, FUNNY CHARACTERS. HERE A TRADITIONAL COLORING BOOK PALETTE IS USED WITH A BLUE SKY AND YELLOW DUCKS.

Skill level: **1**

Materials

Standard-size vitreous glass tiles with the option of stick-on, "googly" eyes
Estimating tile quantities, **see page 11**

COLOR PALETTE

Main panel | Variation

Order of work

1 Start with the eyes: try to make each duck appear as though it is looking at its neighbor. (If using googly eyes, place a circular "blank" tile in the position of the eye, over which you can glue the eye later.)

2 Tile the beaks, laying the top and bottom sections separately.

3 Next place the feet.

4 Make the outline of the body of the ducks curvaceous by using small, nibbling cuts. This will create the softness of the downy feathers.

5 A simple square fill completes the background.

ORDER OF WORK **KEY**

VARIATION: BRIGHT AND VIBRANT

Color variation
An even more vibrant alternative uses a boisterous rainbow palette.

PANEL TRANSFER GRID

Suggested dimensions
To scale and transfer the design follow the techniques described on pages 18–19.
Size of design: 9 x 41¾ in. (23 x 106 cm).

TILE CUTTING AND PLACEMENT GUIDE

MOSAIC 47: FLOWER FAIRY

THIS IS A "FLOWER CHILD" FAIRY WEARING BELLBOTTOMS AND FLOWERS IN HER HAIR. USE SOFTER-TONED, IRIDESCENT TILES TO GIVE HER WINGS A TRANSLUCENT SHIMMER, OR, ALTERNATIVELY, USE MIRROR GLASS. ADD DIAMANTÉ STARS AFTER GROUTING THE FINISHED PIECE TO ADD A TOUCH OF GLITTER.

PANEL TRANSFER GRID

Skill level: **3**

Materials

Standard-size vitreous tiles, diamantés
Estimating tile quantities, **see page 11**

Order of work

1 Establish the strong center-line of the design by carefully placing the eye and face; then move down to create the smooth curve of the upper torso.

2 Next complete the wings: fan the tiles outward from the fairy's back to retain the web feel.

3 Next work on the leaf "tutu." Complete the left-hand leaf first, then work to the right, completing the larger leaves at the top. Next do the leaves that are partly masked by the upper layer.

4 Start with the heart and flower motifs on the bellbottoms, then tile in-between them.

5 The hair is central to the design. If you find doing so many small flowers difficult, then just make fewer, larger ones. The important thing is to cram this area so that it is bursting with flowers.

6 "Ground" the picture by carefully placing the grass along the bottom edge.

7–8 Now cut and place the toadstools (note the tiny pair of wings sticking out from behind the toadstool in the left-hand corner).

9–10 The two areas of background should be tiled with even, curved tile fills that follow the wavy outline.

11–12 Tile the branches of the trees first, then complete the foliage.

13 Place the stars: do the centers first, then the outline where there is one.

14 Finally, fill in the sky.

15 When grouted, add tiny diamanté details around the stars.

Suggested dimensions

To scale and transfer the design follow the techniques described on pages 18–19. Size of design: 33 x 20⅝ in. (84 x 52.5 cm).

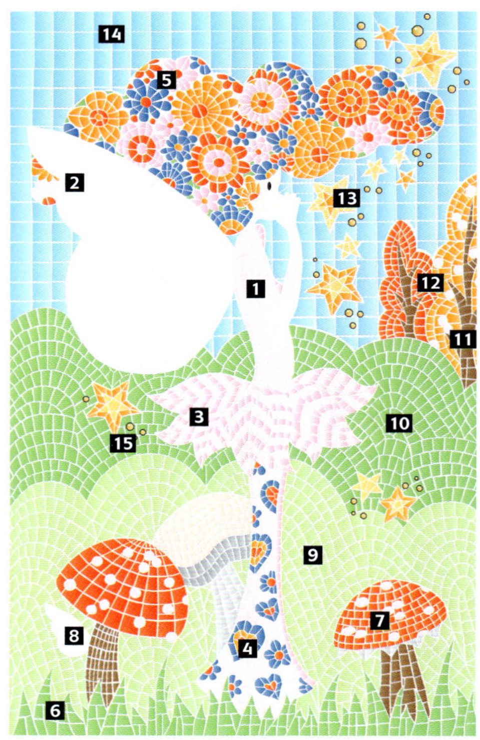

ORDER OF WORK **KEY**

TILE CUTTING AND PLACEMENT GUIDE

COLOR PALETTE

Main panel | Variation

Color variation

This variation uses the same set of colors, but reverses them to make the fairy figure more leaf-like, while turning the background a hotter, "psychedelic" pink.

VARIATION: PSYCHEDELIC

MOSAIC 48:
OWL AT THE WINDOW

A "TROMPE L'OEIL" PIECE, IN WHICH THE SHADOWING ON THE WINDOW FRAME, AND THE OBJECTS IN FRONT OF IT, GIVE A 3-D EFFECT. THE HARVEST MOON GLOWS BEHIND THE STYLIZED OWL WITH ITS BIG, SAUCER-LIKE EYES. THE SPINES OF THE BOOKS ARRANGED ALONG THE WINDOW SILL COULD BE PERSONALIZED WITH A CHILD'S NAME OR THE TITLE OF A FAVORITE BOOK.

Skill level: **2**

Materials

Standard-size vitreous tiles
Estimating tile quantities,
see page 11

ORDER OF WORK **KEY**

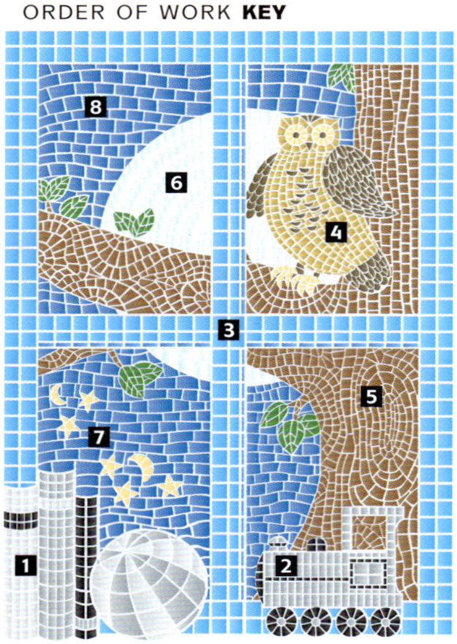

PANEL TRANSFER GRID

Order of work

1 Start by tiling the books and objects along the bottom of the picture. Make them slightly overhang the window sill to give a 3-D feel. The ball is tricky: practice cutting the tiles so that each segment tapers smoothly.

2 With the toy train, begin with the horizontal markings, then the body, finally completing the wheels.

3 Now the window frame: the lighter bulk first, then the darker shade to create the surfaces in shadow. In both cases make sure all edges are laid absolutely straight.

4 Make the eyes of the owl circular and "larger than life." Semicircular cuts provide the effect of feathers; for the plumage work downward filling the wings, breast, and tail. Use angular cuts to create feet and claws.

5 The treetrunk and branches are given a faux wood-grain effect using circular and flowing fills. Alternate slightly different shades of brown to heighten the effect.

6 The moon is oversized—try and use pearlescent tiles of a very light color, rather than pure white tiles.

7 The stars and moons in the bottom left-hand pane are meant to be stickers placed there by a child; keep the shapes simple and fill with bright, flat colors.

8 Finish with the sky using an even fill of the darkest-toned tiles.

VARIATION: MOONLIT

Color variation

This variation extravagantly makes use of gold tiles to give the ghostly luminescence of moonlight.

Suggested dimensions

To scale and transfer the design follow the techniques described on pages 18–19. Size of design: 33 x 23¼ in. (84 x 59 cm).

TILE CUTTING AND PLACEMENT GUIDE

COLOR PALETTE

Main panel | Variation

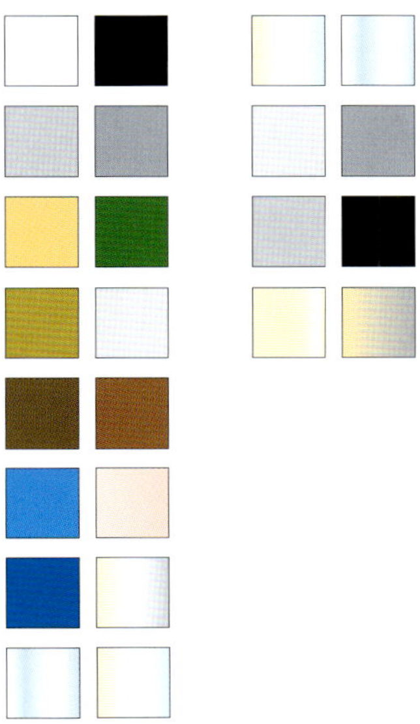

MOSAIC 49: ANIMAL PANEL

THIS IS ANOTHER "STYLIZED" RATHER THAN NATURALISTIC PIECE, CONSISTING OF SIMPLE, INDIVIDUAL PANELS. EACH CONTAINS A TEASING GLIMPSE OF AN ANIMAL. YOU COULD REARRANGE THEIR ORDER OR EXPERIMENT WITH DIFFERENT BACKGROUND COLORS AND FILLS.

Skill level: **2**

Materials

Standard-size vitreous tiles
Estimating tile quantities, **see page 11**

PANEL TRANSFER GRID

Suggested dimensions
To scale and transfer the design follow the techniques described on pages 18–19. Size of design: 25½ x 12¼ in. (64.5 x 31 cm).

ORDER OF WORK **KEY**

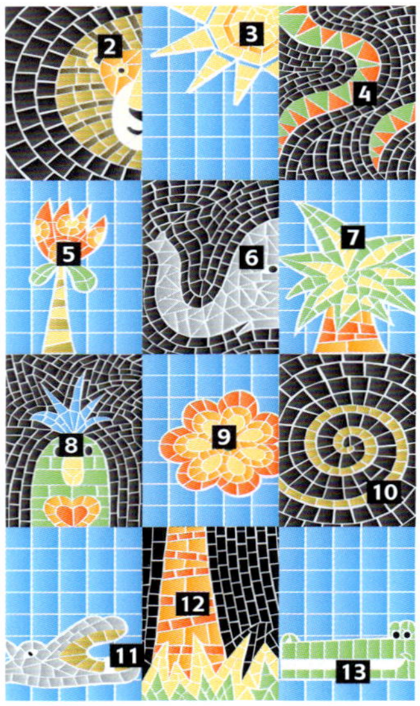

Order of work
Work through each panel one at a time, starting at the top left. If you rearrange the panels, you will need to follow the instructions below in a different order.

1 Lion: place the stripes of the mane along with the eyes, then fill from the center of the face outward, finishing with the flat background.

2 Sun: fill the center of the sun as a flat fill, then lay the surrounding tiles as an outline, before cutting and placing the triangular shards. Again finish with the background.

3 Snakeskin: pre-cut simple triangles in two colors then lay them alternately. Rearrange or nibble the tiles to make narrower triangles so that the snakes curve smoothly.

4 Flower head: cut and place the circular shapes, then fill around with the bright red tiles. The two leaves are symmetrical, pendant shapes. Finally, complete the stem working downward from the flower, tapering tiles in alternate colors.

5 Elephant: place the eye then fill the head in rows that follow the curves of the outline.

6 Palm tree: draw the outline of the leaves carefully, then accurately fill in the central, yellow areas. Use tile pieces of the same width to complete the surrounding green areas. Again, use alternating bands of color for the trunk.

7 Lovebird: draw a vertical center-line and measure from this with a ruler to place the features and markings of the bird exactly to ensure that they are symmetrical.

8 Pomegranate flower: place the motif slightly off-center, and clip the right-hand edge away to provide interest. Work from the center outward.

9 Monkey tail: draw the spiral with a thick pencil—it may take several tries to get it exactly right—then use small, square-shaped bits of tile working out from the center. It helps to taper the edges of the tiles so they fit together to form a curve but with an even space for grout in between each one.

10 Hippo: similar approach to the elephant, but complete the teeth and mouth before the gray fill of the head.

11 Palm tree trunk: keep the shapes sharp and exaggerate the bands on the trunk by using a vivid color. Place them at slightly discordant angles.

12 Crocodile: place simple alternating triangles of white tiles to create the teeth, then use the same white to surround the dark, beady circles of the eyes. For the vibrant green skin, keep the background bright and avoid too dark a tone.

COLOR PALETTE

Color variation

This vibrant alternative uses a bright palette of warm background colors.

VARIATION: WARM PALETTE

TILE CUTTING AND PLACEMENT GUIDE

MOSAIC 50: ELEPHANT FAMILY

THIS FUN FAMILY OF ELEPHANTS WORKS WELL IN A CHILDREN'S PLAYROOM OR NURSERY. THE DESIGN LENDS ITSELF TO A VIBRANT OR QUIRKY COLOR PALETTE. EXPERIMENT BY SWAPPING THE PATTERNS ON THE ELEPHANTS AROUND, OR SIMPLIFYING THEM FURTHER, AS IN THE PINK ELEPHANT.

COLOR PALETTE

Main panel | Variation

Skill level: **4**

Materials

Standard-size vitreous tiles
Estimating tile quantities, **see page 11**

TILE CUTTING AND PLACEMENT GUIDE

VARIATION: NOCTURNAL

Color variation

This gray-scale version gives a moodier, nocturnal feel, but retains the humor of the piece. Find the deepest, jet black tiles to really surround the figures, and for the lighter tones use tiles with a hint of color or pearlescent finish to give a moonlight sheen.

PANEL TRANSFER GRID

Suggested dimensions

To scale and transfer the design follow the techniques described on pages 18–19. Size of design: 11 x 35¾ in. (28 x 91 cm).

Simplify the design

You could simplify any part of this design by using plain fills for the elephants, or enlarging a single motif to fill the whole body.

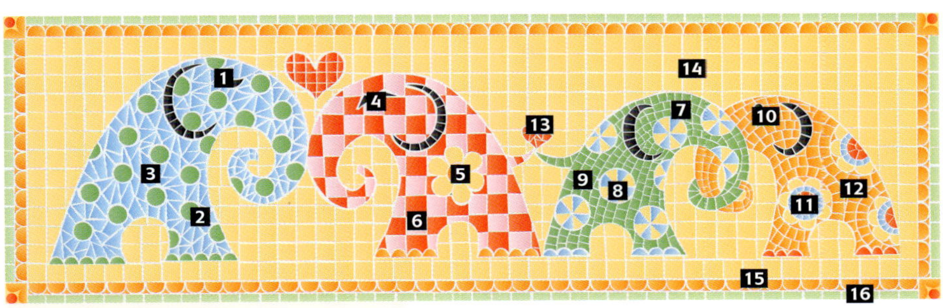

ORDER OF WORK **KEY**

Order of work

1 Start with the first elephant by placing the curve of the ear and carefully positioning the eye.

2 Cut the polka dots from a single tile and place them. Next, do the toenails, also made from cut circles, but split in half.

3 Fill the elephant's body with a crackle pattern of randomly cut tiles.

4 Move on to the second elephant, starting with the eyelashes and the ear—take time to get these precise shapes exact.

5 The circular center of the flower is cut from one tile. The petals are also cut as circles, but with one edge snipped off.

6 Complete the body of the second elephant with a simple checkerboard fill.

7 Now do the next elephant, again eyes and ears first.

8 The large circles are made up of eight triangular segments. Now do the toenails as before.

9 The tile fill for this elephant follows the curve of the body: use smaller pieces, cutting whole tiles into quarters as your starting point.

10 The final elephant! Again ears and eyes first.

11 The flowers are made up of a small, central circular tile surrounded by segments.

12 The tile fill for the final elephant flows around the flowers.

13 The heart provides a focus to the intertwining tails.

14 A checkerboard infill provides the bulk of the background.

15 The semicircles of the inner border echo the elephants' toenails.

16 Lastly, make an outer border of rectangular tiles, with decorative corners if you wish.

INDEX

SUPPLIERS

Artful Crafter, Inc.
741 Lawson Avenue
Havertown, PA 19083
Tel: 1 877 321 2080
www.artfulcrafter.com

D&L Stained Glass Supply, Inc.
4939 North Broadway
Boulder, CO 80304
Tel: 1 800 525 0940
www.dlstainedglass.com

Delphi Creativity Group
3380 East Jolly Road
Lansing, MI 48910
Tel: 1 800 248 2048
www.delphiglass.com

Dick Blick Art Materials
P.O. Box 1267
Galesburg, IL 61402-1267
Tel: 1 800 723 2787
www.dickblick.com

Ed Hoy's International
27625 Diehl Road
Warrenville, IL 60555
Tel: 1 800 323 5668
www.edhoy.com

Firefly Mosaics
1925 Main Street, Suite 4
Ramona, CA 92065
Tel: 1 866 663 2977
www.mosaictile.com

Hakatai Enterprises, Inc.
701 Mistletoe Road
Ashland, OR 97520
Tel: 1 541 552 0855
www.hakatai.com

KP Tiles Mosaic Tile Supplies
1832 Star Batt
Rochester Hills, MI 48309
Tel: 1 248 853 0418
www.kptiles.com

Michael's Arts and Crafts Stores
www.michaels.com

Mosaic Mercantile
P.O. Box 78206
San Francisco, CA 94107
Tel: 1 877 9 MOSAIC
www.mosaicmercantile.com

MosaicSmalti.com
P.O. Box 581
West Harwich, MA 02671
Tel: 1 866 432 5369
www.mosaicsmalti.com

Mosaic Tile Supplies, LLC
100 Anthony Lane
Coldspring, TX 77331
Tel: 1 936 653 8099
www.mosaictilesupplies.com

Pompei Mosaic Tile
11301 Olympic Blvd., Suite 512
West Los Angeles, CA 90064
Tel: 1 310 312 9893
www.pompei-mosaic.com

Vedovato Brothers Inc.
246 East 116th Street
New York, NY 10029
Tel: 1 212 534 2854
www.westchestertile.com

CREDITS

Quarto would like to acknowledge the following:

Page 15 © Fernando Bengoechea/ Beateworks/Corbis

Page 24 © Tim Street-Porter/ Beateworks/Corbis

All other photographs are the copyright of Quarto Publishing plc. While every effort has been made to credit contributors, Quarto would like to apologize should there have been any omissions or errors—and would be pleased to make the appropriate correction for future editions of the book.